Teaching Higher Education
Courses in the FE and Skills Sector

Teaching
Higher Education
Courses in the FE and Skills Sector

Jonathan Tummons

Kevin Orr

Liz Atkins

Los Angeles | London | New Delhi
Singapore | Washington DC

Learning Matters
An imprint of SAGE Publications Ltd
1 Oliver's Yard
55 City Road
London EC1Y 1SP

SAGE Publications Inc.
2455 Teller Road
Thousand Oaks, California 91320

SAGE Publications India Pvt Ltd
B 1/I 1 Mohan Cooperative Industrial Area
Mathura Road
New Delhi 110 044

SAGE Publications Asia-Pacific Pte Ltd
3 Church Street
#10-04 Samsung Hub
Singapore 049483

Editor: Amy Thornton
Development editor: Clare Weaver
Production controller: Chris Marke
Project management: Deer Park Productions, Tavistock
Marketing manager: Catherine Slinn
Cover design: Topics
Typeset by: C&M Digitals (P) Ltd, Chennai, India
Printed by: Henry Ling Limited, at the Dorset Press, Dorchester, DT1 1HD

© Jonathan Tummons, Kevin Orr, Liz Atkins 2013

First published 2013

Library of Congress Control Number: 2013943598

British Library Cataloguing in Publication data

A catalogue record for this book is available from the British Library

ISBN 978 1 44626 746 2 (hbk)
ISBN 978 1 44626 747 9 (pbk)

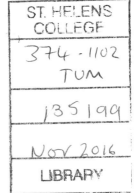

Contents

About the authors

Dr Liz Atkins is a Lecturer and Researcher in Education at the University of Huddersfield. She has taught extensively in both further and higher education on both vocational and teacher education programmes and has also managed provision in which university programmes were taught in FE colleges. She has published widely on issues associated with vocational education and training. Her most recent book, written with Professor Susan Wallace, is *Qualitative Research in Education* (SAGE).

Dr Kevin Orr worked in further education colleges for 16 years before becoming a Senior Lecturer in Education at the University of Huddersfield in 2006. Aside from teaching on a variety of courses, his research interests lie primarily in vocational and further education. Since 2008 he has been co-convenor of the British Educational Research Association's special interest group for post-compulsory and lifelong learning.

Dr Jonathan Tummons worked in further and adult education before moving into higher education. After four years at Teesside University, he has now taken up a post as Lecturer in Education at Durham University. He has researched and published widely on a range of issue relating to learning, teaching and assessment in further and higher education. He is the author of, amongst other books and articles, *Assessing Learning in the Lifelong Learning Sector, Curriculum Studies in the Lifelong Learning Sector,* and *Becoming a Professional Tutor in the Lifelong Learning Sector*, all published by SAGE/ Learning Matters.

Acknowledgements

We would like to thank all of the FE colleagues we have had the privilege of working with during our respective careers in both the further and higher education sectors. We would also like to thank the students we have met, taught, worked alongside and learned with and from, who have undertaken FE in HE and whose experience is the focus of this book.

Introduction

Further education (FE) colleges have long been involved in the provision of higher-level programmes of study, but over recent years – and particularly since incorporation – this has expanded. The provision of higher education (HE) courses within FE colleges constitutes a significant aspect of current moves to expand participation in HE more generally. Over recent years, an increasing number of universities have begun to work with FE colleges in order to offer degree-level education. The scale of provision is considerable: degrees, foundation degrees and certificates are available in an increasing number of subject areas. For staff working in FE colleges, HE in FE provision represents a significant moment of personal and professional development, raising new challenges in terms of teaching and learning strategies, assessment practices and quality assurance systems. In writing this book, we provide an up-to-date account of the key debates and issues that surround the provision of HE courses in FE colleges. This is an account that rests on wider research and scholarship, our own research as academics with an interest in HE in FE, and our own current and past experience as practitioners, both in colleges and in universities.

Each of the chapters in this book has been written so that it stands alone: in this way, the reader can elect either to dip in to the text in order to explore particular key themes, or to read the book from cover to cover. A number of pedagogic activities are included in the text. For the reader who wises to pursue these themes in more depth, references appear at the end of each chapter.

1

College-based higher education and widening participation

By the end of this chapter you will be able to:

- contextualise widening participation in HE in terms of the political agenda;
- understand the academic and organisational implications of offering college-based higher education;
- discuss the new types of HE provision offered in FE;
- describe a broad range of curricula offered under the college-based higher education banner.

Introduction

The term 'widening participation' refers to a broad range of initiatives and activities which have taken place, over time, across both the HE and FE sectors. In terms of college-based higher education, however, it is used to:

> ...denote activities to recruit students from the groups that HEIs have identified as under-represented, and then to ensure their success. These groups may include disabled people, people from a particular cultural or socio-economic background, or even a particular gender.

> (HEA, 2012, online)

Widening participation has been a major theme in government education policy for over a decade. This chapter explores the origins of the widening participation agenda, and considers it in the context of academic concepts of social justice. It explores the political and educational context surrounding widening participation, as well as the debates for and against what has become, for many, a contentious issue. A key aspect of the concerns around widening participation focus on the fact that HE is, like wider society, highly stratified. This means that students studying at higher status institutions (who tend to be more socially and economically advantaged) gain credentials that have greater exchange value than those that other students (who tend to be more disadvantaged) gain from lower status institutions. This is an important point, and one that we shall return to.

While this chapter is focused on widening participation, it is worth pointing out that many of the discourses, or discussions, surrounding widening participation resonate with those surrounding inclusion, which is itself a contested and sometimes controversial subject. Both are concerned with addressing issues of social and educational exclusion. Many of the students who benefit from inclusion policies and practices, or who form part of the widening participation agenda, may be seen to exhibit a range of characteristics associated with social exclusion (such as gender, a lack of credentials, ethnicity, disability, poverty and class), which locates them at the bottom of a highly stratified society. It is important, however, to be aware that within these hierarchies there are *layers* of inclusion and exclusion and not just a simple distinction between inclusion and exclusion (Bathmaker, 2005).

RESEARCH FOCUS   **RESEARCH** FOCUS

Hoelscher et al. (2008, page 149) have identified three goals of widening participation. They argue that two of these (fair access and widening participation to include under-represented groups) are *deeply rooted in notions of social justice*. The term social justice is widely used in education, and most people working in education would argue that they are committed to social justice. So, indeed, would politicians of all persuasions and this is often explicitly reflected in policies which claim to be, for example, *an engine for social justice and equality of opportunity* (DfES, 2006, page 1e). That so many people, often with extremely polarised views, claim a belief in social justice reflects the fact that it is a confused and debated notion, which has no clear definition but is open to many different interpretations and meanings.

Among some of the key authors on this subject, Minogue (1998, page 234) has described it as a *family of ideas* and an *abstract universal*, while MacIntyre (1981, page 234) refers to an *older moral tradition* but also refers to *rival* traditions (page 235), illustrating the conflicting views of the meaning of social justice. Here we explore some of the origins, interpretations and definitions of social justice prior to considering them in the context of equality and inequality in education. The notion of justice, as we understand it in a Western tradition, is ancient and is rooted in both the morality of the early Greek philosophers and ancient Judaeo-Christian texts. Plato and Aristotle, the ancient Greek philosophers, were among the first to debate the notion of justice. They regarded it as a form of morality: in Plato's writings one definition refers to *telling the truth and paying one's debts* (Lee, 1955, page 3). Similarly, early Biblical references to the notion of justice are also related to morality as well as to the concept of *righteousness* (e.g. Amos 5:24). Later, the idea of reciprocity was introduced, as in New Testament teaching that *If any would not work, neither should he eat* (2 Thessalonians 3:10). This notion later appears in work by the leading enlightenment philosopher David Hume (1740: III ii 2, page 318) and, more recently, in work by Minogue (1998, page 258). These notions eventually led to the concepts of deserving and undeserving poor, which originated in Victorian times and which continue to be debated today. Since ancient times, therefore, people have debated exactly what it means to act in a moral way, and what is just or fair and it is from these debates that contemporary ideas around social justice in both education and wider society have developed. Because it is a debated concept, many writers, from Socrates (born 469BC) to more contemporary authors such as Griffiths (2003) advocate a *dialogic* approach to the development of social justice. By this, they mean debating and agreeing ways forward to create a more just and equitable society.

The notion of social justice has particular resonance in education, where there is evidence of significant inequality in terms of the opportunity to access more elite forms of education, which result in greater opportunities well beyond formal education in terms of potential employability and level of income. For this reason, many academics writing about education draw on concepts of social justice. Notable among these is Pierre Bourdieu (see Chapter 3). In addition to academics and those working in education, politicians of all parties have drawn on concepts of social justice as a means of justifying particular policies, particularly those in relation to health and welfare as well as education, since these are the three key areas where there are particular concerns around in/equalities. In England and Wales, for example, more elite forms of education such as public and grammar schools as well as universities, have traditionally been available only to the more afflu-ent or middle class in society and this has led to a situation where whole groups (such as those from lower socio-economic groups or from particular ethnic minorities) have been under-represented in higher education. The widening participation agenda initiated by New Labour sought to address this by including traditionally under-represented groups. However, the agenda has been criticised. In summary, many of the arguments both for and against widening participation use social justice as a form of justification, arguing that certain policies or strategies will either promote social justice or should be abandoned because they are contrary to social justice.

What follows is a summary of some of these debates: it is up to you to decide which arguments are most compelling, and which seem supported with the clearest evidence.

Widening participation: debates for and against

This section begins with a reflective task, designed to help you to consider the merits and weaknesses of each of the debates explored here.

REFLECTIVE TASK

Is it possible to claim that a policy or strategy is socially just if social justice is such a debated concept? Think about your answer and make notes on it. You could also discuss it with a peer or a mentor. Come back to them when you have finished reading the chapter and see whether your ideas have changed.

First, there is the economic argument that the benefits of HE have been exaggerated and that the outcomes for individuals, in terms of potential earnings and job security, are not as significant as politicians suggest. Related to this is the economic argument that 'upward mobility' among large numbers of the population requires an increase in 'middle-class jobs'. While this has happened historically (notably during reconstruction following the Second World War), this is not the case during the current economic crisis. Related to this is the argument – sometimes called elitist – which suggests that to become more competitive the country does not need large numbers of graduates, but rather large numbers of people with highly developed craft and technical skills, such as plumbers or electricians.

Another debate around widening participation has related to those students who access HE through a vocational education route, rather than by taking the more tradi-tional A levels. Some researchers have suggested that students who progress to HE from vocational programmes as a part of the widening participation initiatives tend to experience more academic difficulties in HE. For example, Lawson (2000) in his study of new engineering undergraduates found that A level students, irrespective of grades, had better basic mathematical skills that those holding vocational qualifications, and other research (e.g. see Hoelscher et al., 2008, page 139 and Hoelscher and Hayward, 2008, page 20) has suggested that students with combinations of vocational and academic qualifications are more likely to access HE successfully than those holding only vocational qualifications. Clearly, this research has implications for college-based higher education, which is primarily vocational, in terms of ensuring that appropriate academic support mechanisms are in place to enable students to develop the skills and understandings necessary for success in HE. Since this is expensive, there is a financial implication for colleges, in terms of the provision of intensive academic support as well as the related organisational and academic challenges for both teaching and support staff.

Other arguments have suggested that while HE can provide many advantages to those who access it, the widening participation agenda itself is essentially flawed. For example, research conducted as part of the major Teaching and Learning Research Project (TLRP) suggested that confining policy initiatives to HE would not improve participation because:

> *...much of the debate on access to higher education is based on inaccurate assumptions. Centuries of preferential male access to university have now eroded, and most students are female. Many, too, are from ethnic minorities, while young white men from poorer families are among the least likely to experience higher education. This research has proved that if we allow for the different performance at school of people from varying social backgrounds, they are equally likely to go to university. The policy implication is clear. Improving primary and secondary schools for all is the route to improved participation in higher education.*

> (TLRP, 2008, page 2)

Other arguments which make the case for a flawed process include the contention that higher education institutions (HEIs) are pressured into taking increasing numbers of widening participation students, because they are judged on their commitment to widening participation via the university league tables. The league tables ascribe a 'grade' to institutions based on the numbers of students they do, or do not admit, who fall into the widening participation cohort. This argument goes on to suggest that if HEIs are required to prioritise students perceived to be from certain social groups, this will disadvantage students from social groups which are not prioritised, as there will be fewer places for them to access both generally and at specific institutions.

Finally, there are ongoing arguments about the extent to which the widening participation agenda has been successful in achieving a more meritocratic education system. Some of these arguments suggest that participation has been *increased* but not *widened*, because what has actually happened is that more middle-class young people have been encouraged to apply to universities as a consequence of the agenda, while applications from traditionally under-represented groups have remained relatively unchanged. However, the data on this is open to interpretation and it is equally possible to make a case saying thing that the agenda has been successful in attracting increasing numbers of students from traditionally under-represented backgrounds into HE.

REFLECTIVE TASK

One of the arguments around widening participation is that the agenda can prioritise certain groups who are seen to be more disadvantaged and that this can, in turn, lead to reverse forms of discrimination against young people from more advantaged backgrounds who become unable to access a place in HE not because they do not hold the necessary credentials, but because they do not fit the widening participation criteria. Those who make this argument support it by saying that the criteria used to determine whether a young person falls into the widening participation cohort are arbitrary and unfair. In order to explore these arguments further, read the following scenario and then, with a colleague or fellow student, discuss your responses to the questions that follow.

Paige

Paige was the only child of a father who worked as a care assistant and a mother who was a shop worker. The family lived in social housing on a large post-war development in a city in the English midlands. Paige was four when her mother died of an aggressive form of cancer. Following this, she went to live with her grandmother, who lived nearby, in order to enable her father to continue working. Paige did well at her primary school. This was a feeder school to an 11–16 comprehensive, which had significant problems and had been labelled as 'failing' by both Ofsted and the local authority.

Scenario 1

Paige progressed to the comprehensive, moving from there to the local FE college where she gained a level 3 BTEC Certificate. She subsequently progressed to a foundation degree at the same college. In this scenario, Paige falls into the widening participation cohort.

Scenario 2

Unwilling to allow Paige to attend the comprehensive, Paige's father approached a local independent girls' school. After an entry test, they offered Paige a place with a 90 per cent bursary. Her father committed himself to paying school fees, which, despite the very low rate, represented a huge financial burden to a man earning the minimum wage. Paige achieved three A grade A levels, progressing to an honours degree at a well-regarded university. In this scenario, because she has attended an independent school, Paige does not fall into the widening participation cohort.

Now consider the following questions:

In scenario 2, do the advantages conferred by Paige's secondary education make up for the fact that she comes from a single parent family who have supported her on a very low income? What are the implications for social justice in the context of each of the scenarios? What are the implications for widening participation?

The agenda for widening participation in HE

When we talk about widening participation we tend to refer to the policy begun under New Labour, which had the intention of increasing participation in HE to 50 per cent of all young people by the age of 30 by 2010. However, the idea of widening participation is not new, and if we look back in time we can see other examples of policies intended to achieve this. For example, a University Grants Committee (to support poorer students) was formed as early as 1919, and the notion of equality was embedded in the 1944 Education Act (TLRP 2008), although the outcomes of the 1963 Robbins Report were possibly more far-reaching. The Robbins Report was the outcome of the National Committee of Inquiry into Higher Education. The first principle in its terms of reference stated that: *There should be maximum participation in initial higher education by young and mature students and in lifetime learning by adults, having regard to the needs of individuals, the nation and the future labour market...* it is possible to see echoes of this statement in more recent documents published by New Labour. For example, the 2003 White Paper *The Future of Higher Education* makes a statement of intent to:

- *develop the way we use public funding so as to stimulate greater success and higher quality in teaching, research, knowledge transfer, widening participation and economic and cultural impact on the community;*
- *for all universities and colleges to be committed to fair access for students from all backgrounds, to serving the whole community and to increasing the economic health of their region and the country as a whole;*
- *to improve the economic contribution that universities and colleges make through innovation, improving the skills of the nation and stimulating new businesses in an increasingly competitive world.*

(DfES, 2003, page 92)

Both statements reflect a concern with economic success and a belief that this is directly correlated to the educational levels of the working population. Both also refer to the individual benefits of education, Robbins in the sense of 'individual needs', and New Labour in a context of fairness. Following the Robbins Report (1963) an expansion in the HE sector took place (for example, universities such as York and Warwick were founded in response to this initiative) and polytechnics emerged simultaneously to meet a perceived need for technological skill: it was hoped that this expansion in HE would permit larger numbers of working-class teenagers to access HE (McCulloch, 1994, page 34). Similarly, a significant expansion in HE has taken place since *The Future of Higher Education* was published in 2003, much of which has taken place in FE colleges.

Both initiatives were intended to address the issues related to HE being the preserve of the more affluent and those from higher socio-economic groups. This relationship with social class is historic and has its roots in the Platonic system of education that we have had in England since the Middle Ages. Plato considered the seven liberal arts, or branches of knowledge, the only fit study for free men, defined as those having the authority to vote. For others, mechanical or 'vulgar' pursuits were considered acceptable (Board of Education, 1938, page 403). Thus, in Ancient Greece, a person's place in the social hierarchy determined the nature of the education they received and, for historical reasons, a similar pattern emerged and became embedded in England and Wales. Therefore, different forms of education, training, and ultimately work and life chances, became associated with particular social classes and the policies alluded to above have all attempted to redress this.

The drive to widen participation, which became a key part of New Labour policy, became a political priority after the 'Laura Spence Affair' in 2000. Laura Spence was a comprehensive school pupil from Tyneside who gained five A grade A levels but whose application to Oxford University was rejected. This provoked a media debate about elitism (which became all the more intense when Miss Spence was granted a scholarship to Harvard University): Gordon Brown, then Chancellor of the Exchequer, intervened in the row, which became increasingly polarised. However, irrespective of the rights and wrongs of this affair, it does mark the point at which the Labour government began to take a philosophical position on access to HE. This subsequently entered government policy (o.g. coo *The Future of Higher Education*, 2003) but also became a key aim of quasi-independent organisations such as the Higher Education Funding Council for England (HEFCE) whose website has a banner headline echoing this policy and philosophy and stating that: *Widening access and improving participation in higher education are a crucial part of our mission. Our aim is to promote and provide the opportunity of successful participation in higher education to everyone who can benefit from it. This is vital for social justice and economic competitiveness* (HEFCE, 2012, online).

In addition to tho influcncc of organisations such as IICFCC, the agenda also generated a whole industry in schools and colleges as teachers and lecturers sought to prepare young people who fell into the 'widening participation' category for university and to develop education pathways that would facilitate this. This included the introduction of initiatives and schemes such as AimHigher and Gifted and Talented, both of which sought to identify young people from the widening participation cohort who might be supported to access HE.

While the focus of the widening participation agenda has consistently been on enabling young people to access HE – something which is reflected in this chapter – one of the consequences has been an increase in the numbers of *mature* students, something which is particularly evident in college-based higher education programmes.

Rationale

The rationale behind the widening participation agenda was twofold and sought to meet both ideological and economic aims. Both were well intentioned, although, as we have seen, the policy was contentious and, as this chapter goes on to discuss, it also had some unintended consequences. In ideological terms the policy was founded in a belief that HE should be re-structured around a philosophy of equality. Therefore, it aimed to raise aspirations and offer opportunities to groups of young people who had traditionally been under-represented in HE. This included those from lower socio-economic groups as well as young people from specific ethnic minority groups and those with disabilities. These young people would then access HE, and through this, professional, graduate occupations associated with higher incomes. Research has shown that a degree carries considerable economic benefits. For example, at the time of the introduction of £3000 fees threshold in 2006, Universities UK undertook research into the lifetime value of a degree in comparison to A levels. Their data suggested *that there are significant economic benefits (as well as substantial non-financial advantages) to obtaining a degree and these amount to an additional £160,000 over a working lifetime compared with an individual with two or more A-levels* (Universities UK, 2007, page 1). Although this would vary according to the type of degree, this sort of potential benefit underpinned a policy which was intended to lead to a more meritocratic society in which people achieved success based on *a*bility rather than *di*sability, social class or ethnicity. In economic terms, at a time when the UK economy was beginning to lag behind those of some emerging economies, such as China, the policy was intended to create a more highly educated, and so more competitive, workforce. Making the UK more competitive in the global economy would generate greater profits for the country as a whole and, ultimately, lead to raised standards of living for all. However, as illustrated in the section above on *Widening participation: debates for and against*, these findings have been subject to criticism.

Political context

It is important to be aware that the widening participation agenda does not refer to a single policy, but to a multitude of policies and initiatives which have influenced both FE and HE over time. In fact, FE experienced significant changes as a result of the 1997 Kennedy Report *Learning Works: widening participation in further education,* which made recommendations that resulted in large numbers of students who had not previously accessed FE – including the significantly disadvantaged, the disabled and those with special educational needs – beginning to participate. The impact on college-based higher education, in terms of increased numbers of students and the organisational changes which have followed it, are comparable to those which took place earlier in response to the Kennedy Report and form part of the ongoing changes which have influenced FE over the past 25 years.

The philosophical position and justification for the widening participation agenda is important, but it is at least equally important to note that the initiative was also driven by perceived economic imperatives. This is reflected in the 'key points' listed in the policy document *The Future of Higher Education* (2003) which justified the various aspects of the policy (including the introduction of university fees) on the grounds that, among other things:

- *Higher Education must expand to meet rising skill needs;*
- *The social class gap between those entering university remains too wide;*
- *Universities need stronger links with business and the economy (DfES, 2003, page 4).*

The importance of education as a means of meeting the country's economic needs has been recognised for many years – a good example is the quote from the Robbins Report, used earlier, which refers to the necessity of meeting the needs of *the future labour market*. However, there is a point in time at which economic policy became the driver for education policy, and this is usually acknowledged as being 1976, when James Callaghan made his speech 'Towards a National Debate' at Ruskin College, Oxford. This called for a change in approach to education, arguing that *there is no virtue in producing socially well-adjusted members of society who are unemployed because they do not have the skills* (Callaghan, 1976). Since this time, perceived economic needs – for example, for technically skilled workers – have had a significant influence on education policy. In terms of the widening participation agenda, although part of the justification has been that a system which is not fully inclusive and does not offer equal opportunities to all is contrary to social justice, another justification is that higher levels of education are essential for all in the context of a globalised, increasingly high skills economy.

These economic arguments have been made in the education policies of both New Labour and the Coalition government. They imply that unless a person has a high level of education (at least level 3 and ideally higher education) then they will find it very difficult to compete in the jobs market and the country as a whole will not have sufficient skilled workers, such as technicians and engineers, to compete with the major emerging economies such as China and Brazil. These imperatives have generated a broad range of policies across all phases of education, as well as over-arching initiatives such as widening participation. Given that the concept of widening participation is largely subscribed to across the political spectrum, it is likely that it will remain in place as an ongoing initiative for the foreseeable future. However, the current age of austerity has implications for how the agenda is put into practice. For example, the AimHigher programme, established by New Labour, worked through partnerships across England, which involved schools and universities in supporting young people from non-traditional backgrounds to consider and prepare for HE. It was, however, very expensive and the programme was formally closed in 2011 as a result of government spending cuts. Following this, the responsibility for widening participation moved to universities, thus relieving the taxpayer of the direct cost of programmes such as AimHigher. The Coalition committed to ensuring that widening participation for students from all backgrounds remained a *key strategic objective for all higher education institutions* (2011, page 56) and with the publication of the White Paper *Higher Education: Students at the Heart of the System* (BIS, 2011) placed 'much tougher' requirements on universities to ensure fair access and widening participation. However, the same White Paper also introduced a new policy that removed the restriction on universities to recruit only limited numbers of students where applicants held high grades of AAB at A level or above. This has raised concerns that competition for these students will conflict with universities' strategic aims to widen participation, particularly since many of the applicants who fall into the widening participation cohort have lower or alternative entry profiles.

Academic and organisational implications

The policy to widen participation in *HE* had significant implications for *FE* in the short, medium and longer term, and generated many opportunities for development. The implications for FE colleges fell into two broad categories – academic and organisational. In terms of organisational implications, it quickly became apparent that the vast majority of FE students fell into the widening participation cohort. Therefore, colleges increasingly began to develop clear pathways through their existing (mainly vocational) curricula to provide the possibility of progression to HE irrespective of the student's starting point in college. This, together with other government initiatives associated with improving the esteem in which vocational education is held, led to an increase in the number of 'broad vocational' (i.e. vocationally *orientated* and mainly classroom based) as 'progression routes' (DfES 2005; 2006; 2007; DCFS 2008) to more advanced levels of vocational training as part of the widening participation agenda. Thus, it may be seen that the implications of the widening participation agenda were not limited to HE programmes, but filtered down and had significant implications for teachers and young people in schools and colleges, particularly those concerned with the 14–19 phase of education. Other organisational implications are financial in nature: the increased numbers of HE students require accommodation, and their needs and profiles are very different to those of 16–19 students. Consequently, although these new students brought significant financial rewards, many colleges have invested huge sums of money in the development of dedicated HE centres.

A significant academic implication of the widening participation agenda has been the need for teachers in FE to reconcile the different approaches and philosophies to teaching and learning which are found in the HEIs that validate the programmes they deliver, with those in FE. These are very different. HE has traditionally been a place which has sought to develop and extend knowledge and understanding. Therefore, the prevailing philosophy in HE is one of the pursuit of academic excellence. In contrast, while FE has provided technical excellence in terms of occupational skills, it has also catered for large numbers of students who have had unsuccessful school careers and so sought a different kind of education in a different kind of setting. The necessity of meeting the additional needs of these more vulnerable students, as well as other pressures, policies and societal changes, has led to a prevailing philosophy in FE which is concerned with nurturing. While these two philosophies are very different, they are not incompatible: there are, however, tensions between them which have particular implications for the delivery of college-based higher education and which are discussed in more detail in Chapter 2, The HE ethos.

New methods of HE provision

Although HE has been a feature of FE for many years, traditionally most colleges tended to focus on a small number of programme areas. Key among these has been teacher education, where colleges have, for many years, offered part-time, in-service training for new teachers in the sector. However, the widening participation agenda has led to significant expansion. This became accelerated following the introduction of foundation degrees and the publication of subsequent plans by the government to allow FE colleges to validate their own foundation degrees rather than offering them in partnership with a university.

Thus, the widening participation agenda, together with a wide range of other policy initiatives related to higher and vocational education, have been catalysts for the introduction of a broad range of new types of programme to FE. This has included provision such as foundation degrees (introduced in 2001), ePart-time courses, top-up programmes, many of which developed as a consequence of foundation degree graduates wanting to progress to honours degrees, and more extensive use of franchised programmes, as FE colleges have developed closer – and more equal – relationships with the HEIs who are able to validate the new programmes for which they are experiencing a demand.

The way in which franchised programmes operate varies from programme to programme and institution to institution. Broadly speaking, there is a spectrum at one end of which an HEI writes and validates a programme, which is offered by a partner college, with the HEI retaining full academic and quality control. Students enrolled on this type of programme often remain students of the HEI, and this has implications for where the funding flows – to the HEI who then pay the college a fee for each student. At the other end of the spectrum, an HEI may agree to validate a programme and offer some Quality Assurance support, but almost all aspects of the programme will remain under the control of the college. In this case, students are likely to be enrolled only at the college, which will draw down the student funding and pay the HEI for its services. This latter approach has become increasingly common in recent years. Some partnerships have also moved to a consortium model, in which each member has an equal say and degree of control over the management of the programme.

These changes have altered relationships between colleges and HEIs with colleges increasingly taking the 'driving seat'. Previously, when colleges were dependent on HEIs to validate programmes for relatively small numbers of students, this placed the college in a somewhat unequal relationship. Increased demand for the types of programme colleges are able to offer have, however, brought significant numbers of new students together with significant financial rewards and HEIs have increasingly been competing to work in partnership with colleges. This competition has placed colleges in a much stronger position, particularly in terms of negotiations over the ways in which programmes are financed and how any profits are managed. This is illustrated in the case of Osborne College, below.

CASE STUDY

Osborne College had a strong reputation across the North East for its Arts and Drama provision. Following the introduction of foundation degrees in 2001, it approached County University, with whom it already delivered a Certificate in Education in-service programme, and negotiated the development of a partnership in which County would validate foundation degrees in Art and Drama Studies and Osborne would develop and deliver the programmes. This led to the development of top-up programmes introduced in 2003 (Art) and 2004 (Drama Studies). The college subsequently worked with County University to develop and deliver foundation degrees in a broad range of other subjects including Fashion Design, Early Childhood Studies and Teacher Training. In 2008, Osborne College also established a relationship with Westshire University in order to develop its engineering provision. Managers from Westshire suggested that they could offer some of the existing programmes validated by County at increased profits to Osborne. This was a factor in the annual financial negotiations, which took place between Osborne and the HEIs. As a result, Osborne College moved Teacher Training to Westshire, but also came to a more profitable agreement with County regarding the other programmes.

REFLECTIVE TASK

Do you know when the programmes you teach on were introduced? To what extent did they form a response to this period of reform in FE and HE and the introduction of the widening participation agenda?

College-based higher education curricula

The introduction of these new types of programme has led to a broadening of the college-based higher education curricula. However, as discussed in Chapter 3, this has remained highly vocational, reflecting the broader mission of FE which, according to Lingfield (BIS, 2012, page 2), includes Vocational FE and HE studies. Therefore, although the curriculum is broader than it used to be at HE level it continues to mirror the post-16 curriculum in the type of programmes it offers. In addition, college-based higher education has come to encompass programmes which, rather than being academic or vocational, might more properly be described as occupational. This includes provision such as NVQs and related competency-based qualifications at higher levels (4/5) as well as professional credentials such as the Association of Accounting Technicians (AAT) qualifications.

Changes in funding for HE programmes, introduced in the 2011 White Paper, prioritise so-called STEM subjects (Science, Technology, Engineering and Medicine). This means that, over time, we are likely to see a contraction in humanities-based programmes and an expansion in STEM programmes. This also has implications for college-based higher education, as vocational engineering and technology programmes are a strength of the

FE sector generally, and it seems likely that many colleges may seek to capitalise on this change in the funding priorities by expanding these programmes. This provides an opportunity for expansion of college-based higher education, particularly since the subject areas which have recently experienced funding *cuts* are, with the exception of FE teacher training programmes, offered largely by universities rather than as college-based higher education.

A SUMMARY OF KEY POINTS

During this chapter we have looked at the following key issues:

> Understandings of widening participation are rooted in concepts of social justice, but also strongly premised on economic imperatives and needs. There are tensions between these two competing priorities.

> Widening participation is not a single policy, but a broad agenda rooted in many policies and initiatives over time and across sectors and promoted by educational bodies and bureaucracies as well as by government.

> Widening participation has had a major impact on college-based higher education with increased numbers of students, a broader curriculum and, perhaps most significantly, greater autonomy for colleges.

> The widening participation agenda is *deeply rooted in notions of social justice* (Hoelscher et al., 2008, page 149). However, some of the outcomes of the initiative have been criticised for being unjust.

This chapter has shown that the widening participation agenda, while premised on understandings of social justice, is also driven by national and global economic imperatives. It is an initiative that has had a significant influence on college-based higher education, most specifically in terms of the broadening of the curriculum, and in increases in the numbers of students enrolled on HE programmes in FE institutions. Although the way in which the agenda has been implemented has altered as governments and financial priorities have changed, it remains firmly embedded at the heart of HE policy. However, it does seem likely that the tension between the £9000 fees threshold and the freedom universities now have to admit unlimited numbers of AAB candidates may lead to unintended conflicts and consequences as HEIs attempt to reconcile the requirement to maintain fair access with the imperative to attract funding from 'extra' students. These remain to be seen, but changes in funding priorities and the Coalition's explicit commitment to expanding college-based higher education certainly mean that it will continue to be a significant area of investment in years to come.

Branching options

Reflection

As you look back over this chapter, think about which of the arguments and debates around widening participation seem the most powerful, as well as those which seem weaker or flawed. Talk with colleagues at work or with other students and compare your views. Is what you do promoting social justice? How can your programme help to overcome some of the social inequalities alluded to in this chapter?

Analysis

At the beginning of this chapter you were asked whether it is possible to claim that a policy or strategy is socially just if social justice is such a debated concept? Have your ideas changed as you have read this chapter? If so, how or why have they changed. How can an understanding of social justice and its implications for your students contribute to your own professional knowledge or challenge your professional practice?

Research

Notions of social justice are interwoven throughout thinking and research around all forms of education. Much of the research which has been undertaken into widening participation can be found at the site of the *furtherhigher project*, based at the University of Sheffield and available at: www.sheffield.ac.uk/furtherhigher. Look this up and read some of the findings: how does this relate to your own professional practice? How might it inform your practitioner research?

REFERENCES REFERENCES REFERENCES REFERENCES REFERENCES

Bathmaker, A-M. (2005) Hanging in or shaping a future: defining a role for vocationally related learning in a 'knowledge' society', *Journal of Education Policy,* 20 (1): 81–100.

Board of Education (1938) *Report of the Consultative Committee on Secondary Education with Special Reference to Grammar Schools and Technical High Schools* (Spens Report). London: HMSO.

Callaghan, J. (1976) *Towards a National Debate,* speech given at Ruskin College, Oxford, 18 October 1976 available online at: http://education.guardian.co.uk/thegreatdebate/story/0,9860,574645,00.html (accessed 03/06/2013).

Committee on Higher Education, *Higher Education,* Report of the Committee appointed by the Prime Minister under the Chairmanship of Lord Robbins 1961–63 (The Robbins Report), October 1963, Cmnd. 2154.

Department for Business, Innovation and Skills (BIS) (2011) *Higher Education: Students at the Heart of the System.* London: The Stationery Office.

Department for Business, Innovation and Skills (BIS) (2012) *Professionalism in Further Education* (The Lingfield Report). London: The Stationery Office.

Department for Children, Schools and Families (2008) *Promoting Achievement, Valuing Success: A Strategy for 14–19 Qualifications.* Norwich: The Stationery Office.

Department for Education and Skills (2003) *The Future of Higher Education.* London: The Stationery Office.

Department for Education and Skills (2005) *14–19 Education and Skills.* Annesley: DfES Publications.

Department for Education and Skills (2006) *Further Education: Raising Skills, Improving Life Chances.* Norwich: The Stationery Office.

Department for Education and Skills (2007) *Raising Expectations: Staying in Education and Training post-16.* Norwich: The Stationery Office.

Griffiths, M. (2003) *Action for Social Justice in Education*. Maidenhead: Open University Press.

HEA (2012) *Widening Participation.* Available online at: www.heacademy.ac.uk/Widening_participation/ (accessed 03/06/13).

HEFCE (2012) *Widening Participation.* Available online at: www.hefce.ac.uk/whatwedo/wp/ (accessed 03/06/13).

Hoelscher, M. and Hayward, G. (2008) *'Degrees of Success' – Working Paper 3: Analysing Access to HE for Students with Different Educational Backgrounds: Preliminary Descriptive Results.*

Available online at: www.tlrp.org/project%20sites/degrees/documents/Working_Paper_3_MH_ GH_final2.doc (accessed 23/08/2008).

Hoelscher, M., Hayward,G., Ertl, H. and Dunbar-Goddet, H. (2008) The transition from vocational education and training to HE: a successful pathway? *Research Papers in Education,* 23 (2): 139–51.

Hume, D. (1740/2000) *A Treatise of Human Nature* (David Fate Norton and Mary J. Norton eds) Oxford: Oxford University Press.

Kennedy, J. (1997) *Learning Works: Widening Participation in Further Education* (The Kennedy Report). Coventry: FEFC.

Lawson, D. (2000) Vocational education as preparation for university engineering mathematics, *Engineering, Science and Education Journal*, 9 (2): 89–92.

Lee, D. (1955/1987) *Plato: The Republic.* London: Penguin Books.

MacIntyre, A. (1981) *After Virtue: A Moral Theory.* London: Duckworth.

McCulloch, G. (1994) *Educational Reconstruction: The 1944 Education Act and the Twenty First Century.* London: Woburn Press.

Minogue, K. (1998) Social Justice in Theory and Practice in D. Boucher and P. Kelly (eds) *Social Justice from Hume to Walzer.* London: Routledge.

TLRP (2008) *Widening Participation in Higher Education: A Commentary by the Teaching and Learning Research Programme.* Available online at: www.tlrp.org/pub/documents/HEcomm.pdf (accessed 03/06/13).

Universities UK (2007) *Research Report: The Economic Benefits of a Degree.* Available online at: http://www.universitiesuk.ac.uk/Publications/Documents/research-gradprem.pdf last accessed 04/12/12.

2

The HE ethos – creating a university within a college

By the end of this chapter you will be able to:

- describe the key characteristics of an 'HE ethos' in college-based higher education;
- describe the values associated with HE and outline the ways in which you demonstrate these in your professional practice;
- discuss ways in which the 'HE in FE' ethos is distinct from that in universities;
- describe strategies for developing academic and intellectual spaces for your HE students.

Introduction

A concern of professionals involved in the delivery of HE programmes in a college context is ensuring that their programmes have an appropriate 'HE ethos'. Indeed, you may well have discussed with colleagues strategies for promoting an HE ethos on your own programmes. However, although there are expectations that organisations and individual lecturers will promote an HE ethos it can be difficult to 'pin down' exactly what this means. Intuitively perhaps, we are aware that there are significant differences in the way students are taught in FE and the way in which they are taught in HE. Part of this might be attributed to age differences. Many FE students are young people, while a majority of college-based HE students are mature adults. However, the HE ethos relates to more than this, and includes characteristics as diverse as the approach to teaching and learning, resourcing and infrastructure. This means that the ethos on an HE programme is likely to be quite different to that on non-HE programmes, even where students on the FE programmes may be adults intending to progress to HE – for example, students on Access programmes. Developing such an ethos is a concern at macro as well as micro levels. At a macro, national level, HEFCE (who directly fund many college-based HE programmes) actively seek to promote an HE ethos in college-based higher education (see, for example, work by Weatherald and Moseley (2003) which reports on a major HEFCE initiative to support HE in FE). Also at a national level the development of an HE ethos is a concern of the Higher Education Academy (HEA), whose mission is to *champion excellent learning and teaching in higher education* (HEA, 2012: online), as well as of the Quality Assurance Agency (QAA) who are responsible for *safeguarding standards and improving the quality of UK higher education* (QAA, 2013) and who regard the promotion of an appropriate ethos as being one of the features of good quality HE. At a local level, reflecting these national imperatives, the development of a *mature HE culture and ethos* is also seen as a high priority by the management of a majority of large- and medium-sized FE institutions (King et al., 2010, page 34), as well as by the teachers and lecturers whose professional practice is focused in this area.

So, what is an HE ethos? The HEA has published a report on this (Jones, 2006), while HEFCE and QAA make reference to a higher education ethos in institutional reports and a wide range of other documents on their websites. Broadly speaking, these publications suggest that the HE ethos relates to establishing the values and practices which effectively support students on HE programmes, while also enhancing their overall experience. Inevitably, much of this relates to how HE 'feels', something that is qualitatively different to the way in which FE 'feels'. In this chapter, we explore the different characteristics that create this 'feel', and discuss some of the issues experienced by lecturers working in college-based HE as they try to promote an ethos which is 'characteristically HE' (Burns, 2007).

REFLECTIVE TASK

How HE feels different to FE

Discuss with your mentor, or a peer or colleague, how HE *feels* different to FE. Try and identify specific differences and make a note of these. You could consider, for example:

- Expectations
- Students
- Teaching practice
- Assessment practices
- Curriculum
- Scholarship
- Quality Assurance

We will return to this later in the chapter.

RESEARCH FOCUS   RESEARCH FOCUS

FE, reflecting its 'Cinderella' status, is significantly under-researched in comparison to other phases and areas of education. College-based higher education in particular has received very little attention from academics. The most significant project in the 2000s has been *FurtherHigher*, led by academics at the University of Sheffield, which ran from 2006–8. Many of the published outcomes from this study relate to government policies on college-based higher education, an area that has remained in a state of flux since the time the project was undertaken. Other work in the study focused on the student experience, and on the different approaches to teaching and learning in FE and HE. Other research relating to college-based higher education has tended to focus on the contribution college-based HE makes to the wider sector (e.g. see Crozier et al., 2008; Ainley, 2008; Gallacher, 2006) as well as on issues of class and in/equalities in HE (e.g. see Clancy and Goastellec, 2007; Moreau and Leathwood, 2006). There is a dearth of research exploring the ethos of HE in FE. Among the very limited work in this area is the study by Jones (2006) who draws on earlier research (Weatherald and Moseley, 2003) to propose a four-dimensional typology of characteristics that might describe the HE ethos. These dimensions include: teaching and learning; symbolic aspects of HE (such as graduation ceremonies); infrastructural context (meaning the physical environment such as the HE centres established by many FE colleges); and student engagement. Jones argues that in terms of teaching and learning it is not enough for lecturers to make students aware of the different expectations placed on them at HE level, but that it is also necessary to enable them to move beyond directed forms of learning to the autonomous and independent learning which is characteristic of HE and which is associated with concepts of 'deep' as opposed to 'surface' learning. His reference to student engagement relates to activities beyond engagement with a programme, including the social aspects of HE, which most university students are involved with, such as the Students Union and a variety of clubs and societies.

Creating an HE ethos based on this typology presents some challenges, not least because of the relatively small numbers undertaking programmes in many colleges, resulting in significant practical difficulties in, for example, establishing a broad range of clubs and societies. It should also be noted that many mature students, whether undertaking HE in a college or a university, may not wish to engage with social activities which are largely aimed at young undergraduates. In addition, there are cultural differences between FE and HE, particularly in the approaches to teaching and learning, which are acknowledged by Jones and which may influence the HE ethos, particularly where lecturers teach across HE and FE levels. These differences are associated with the greater structure and more supportive environment in FE, approaches which in some organisations are also utilised on HE programmes. Superficially then, in these cases, it may appear that a college-based setting is not encouraging independent learning and thus not promoting an appropriate HE ethos. However, other work argues that this type of approach is one of the key strengths of college-based higher education and implies that it is indicative of an understanding of the specific needs of the learners who access HE in college-based settings. For example, Cockburn (2007, page 19) has proposed a model illustrating the differences in teaching, learning and assessment between 'HE in FE' and 'HE in HE' (see Table 2.1). His study implies that the students accessing college-based higher education require a more structured approach, commonly associated with FE, but different to HE, to enable them to develop skills necessary for the 'deep' and autonomous learning that Jones (2006, page 3) regards as a key characteristic of HE.

Table 2.1 The differences in teaching, learning and assessment between 'HE in FE' and 'HE in HE' (Source: Cockburn, 2007, page 19)

HE in HE	HE in FE
*low support	*high support
*independent learning	*structured andragogy
*academic to holistic	*holistic to academic
*assessment: traditional academic	*assessment: traditional academic

Data from Cockburn's study (2007, page 18) suggested that some staff not only acknowledge fundamental differences in the ethos between HE in HE and HE in FE, but see a particular value in what might be described as an 'HE in FE ethos', reflecting a specific type of provision which possesses its own positive qualities. This perspective, also seen in other studies, has led to suggestions that college-based HE staff may consciously be offering a 'different experience' to their students based on their understanding of the specific needs of those they recruit as well as an intention to *market HE in FE as a truly distinctive experience* (Burkill et al., 2008, page 329).

Many of the differences which generate a distinctive ethos in college-based higher education appear to focus on the cultural dissimilarities in approaches to teaching and learning mentioned earlier. However, despite the imperatives to develop an HE ethos in college-based higher education, it is evident that the way in which this is interpreted varies significantly from institution to institution. For example, variations in teaching and learning culture between colleges were highlighted by Bathmaker et al. (2008) who found conflicting views and practices in research conducted as part of the *Further-Higher* project. This included one college in which staff provided extensive individual support and bridging programmes as part of a highly structured approach, while in a similar institution:

> [HE tutors] were often critical of the supportive structures of teaching and learning in further education, such as open door policies for student support, the extensive use of formative assessment and the availability of numerous assessment opportunities on some vocational pathways: a set of practices ('spoon feeding') considered at odds with the demands of higher education and therefore equally inappropriate on courses preparing students for these levels.

> (Bathmaker et al., 2008, page 134)

These differences in the approach to teaching and learning seem to suggest that, in terms of Jones's typology, while there may be broad similarities between organisations offering college-based higher education, there will also be significant differences. The differences will be attributable to the values and culture pertaining to each individual institution, and will be part of what makes it distinctive, something that has been acknowledged by HEFCE (2009, page 1).

The tensions between different teaching practices, such as those alluded to by Bathmaker et al., and those between the imperative to develop an HE ethos, and the suggestion that FE should, and does, have its own distinctive HE in FE ethos, reflect the conflicting views and priorities of those involved in HE, from governmental policy makers to lecturers in colleges and universities. These tensions are also reflective of the paucity of research in this area, demonstrating a need to undertake further studies which will help us to understand more fully what happens in college-based higher education, who accesses it and why, and what their particular needs and motivations are. Undertaking such research will help to inform practice in the sector, ultimately contributing to improved experiences and outcomes for students.

Physical spaces and resources

In terms of Jones's (2006) four-dimensional typography, this section refers to the infrastructural context. A key aspect of this is that there should be clear demarcation between HE and FE where these are taking place within the same campus. Many colleges have established dedicated HE centres as part of the drive to develop an HE ethos. Some of these are to be found on a separate campus, while others are co-located on a mixed FE/HE campus and others are co-located in buildings which also cater for FE students. To a great extent, the type of infrastructure depends on factors such as whether the college was formed as part of a merger or whether, historically, it was a multi-site institution, as well as the numbers of HE students it enrols and the extent of capital investment. In terms of developing a distinct HE ethos, the ideal is often seen to be locating HE students on a separate campus. However, apart from the financial challenges presented by making such a major investment, there is a key question which deserves an answer: what degree of separateness do the HE students actually *want* and is it possible that some students will be 'put off' the college if they are to be located separately in a building which has all the mystique of a university? In other words, is it possible that locating HE on a different campus might generate more barriers to learning for some students? Is this something that you could usefully explore in your own institution?

Irrespective of location, the type of accommodation needs to be appropriate to creating an HE ethos. HE students increasingly expect the highest possible standards in the facilities they use. This expectation is largely driven by an increasingly marketised sector in which students, not unreasonably, see themselves as paying customers. Therefore, this engenders high expectations of the institution including the belief that aspects of the infrastructure such as decor, furniture and equipment, as well as teaching and learning resources will be well maintained if not new, and appropriate to the needs of the students using it.

Learning resources which adequately support autonomous learning are another key feature of HE, so have a significant place in promoting an HE ethos in college-based higher education. The most important learning resource any institution has is its teachers and lecturers. Your role in promoting an HE ethos is discussed elsewhere in this chapter, but is broadly related to your professional and academic credibility and the ways in which you develop this, through CPD and scholarship. In addition, you are the person who will develop a whole range of resources (for example, lectures, tutorials, seminars, structured activities and discussions), which will support HE teaching and learning in your discipline. It is critical to be aware of this: all too often professionals assume that teaching in HE is limited to 'lecturing'. However, while the approach and ethos are very different to FE, there is no excuse not to use creative and imaginative approaches where these will facilitate students to achieve the desired outcomes. For example, telling students how to undertake a literature review for an assignment is likely to be far less productive than asking them to review three or four relevant publications in small groups based on specific criteria and using their feedback to guide critical discussion.

Other, centrally provided learning resources can be broadly split into three categories: ICLT, specialist resources and library resources such as books and journals. Access to first-class library and ICLT facilities forms a significant aspect of the HE ethos. All institutions now have their own Virtual Learning Environment (VLE), although these vary in accessibility and individual organisations make use of a whole raft of diverse, new and emerging technologies. The opportunities for learning through the use of ICLT are clearly boundless and increasingly integrate the use of social networking sites such as Facebook and Twitter. Most institutions have Twitter feeds for example, and an HE-specific feed offers an opportunity to draw students' attention to special events, research and student and staff achievements – in other words, to promote an HE ethos.

More traditional texts and journals form both a practical and a symbolic means of generating an HE ethos. Practical because they hold the disciplinary and research knowledge that students need to acquire to successfully complete their HE programme and symbolically because the scholarship which is such an important part of the HE culture is reflected in these publications. The value of excellent library facilities in promoting independent learning, and thus an HE ethos, cannot be overstated. It is no accident that we describe students as *reading* for a degree. Thus, inadequate facilities will mean that independent learning is not promoted and that students' access to this important part of the HE culture is limited, both of which have significant implications for their outcomes and progression. In times of economic austerity library budgets have formed part of wider institutional economies in many organisations. Identifying creative and effective strategies for promoting wider reading in the face of this is one of the very current challenges facing HE tutors.

REFLECTIVE TASK

The argument is often made that college-based HE students can access university libraries, either because they are enrolled on a university validated programme or through local or regional reciprocal agreements. However, the reality is that this rarely happens. Students may be daunted by visiting a university, they may not be able to afford the transport or they may not have the time. They often also fail to realise that there is a much broader range of reading than the key texts identified on a reading list. So, what strategies can you utilise to overcome this and promote an HE ethos by facilitating access to a wider range of reading for students?

Discuss this with a peer or colleague and write down your ideas: try to identify three *realistic* suggestions, which, over time, you could integrate into your professional practice. For example, you may have books or equipment of your own which you are able to take into classes occasionally for demonstration purposes; not all students may be aware of the many different sources of second-hand academic texts and equipment and closer liaison with library staff may also generate a range of suggestions for ways in which you could provide a broader range of resources.

The expectations of HE institutions

The expectations of partner HE institutions are often superficially almost entirely related to meeting quality assurance requirements; this means that they are closely related to pedagogic issues such as teaching and assessment. For example, do students receive a similar teaching experience to that on offer at the university? Are the assessment judgements made on students' work the same as those which would be made by university tutors? These issues are critical for the university as well as the college on university-validated programmes, since the university will be deemed to be at fault if any quality issues arise, and this is particularly pertinent to those programmes which are subject to external quality assurance processes, such as Ofsted inspection, as well as internal and QAA Audits. These concerns, therefore, inform the expectations that the HE institution has of the organisation which delivers its programme, although these are often mediated by the staff team directly involved in the delivery and management of a specific programme. However, engagement with those QA and quality evaluation (QE) processes, particularly in terms of the pedagogical approach, and student involvement with the wider programme, provide significant opportunities for promoting an HE ethos. These include the opportunities they offer for sharing best practice and generating new ideas with colleagues from the HE institution, as well as implementing and developing ideas and suggestions arising from student participation in QA and QE processes.

Intellectual and academic spaces: creating an HE ethos

Creating an HE ethos in a college context is, as we have seen, related to teaching and learning, symbolic aspects of HE, infrastructural context and student engagement. Thus, it is partly related to location and physical resourcing of the programme. A significant, if more abstract aspect of creating an HE ethos, however, is the development of intellectual and academic 'space'. This does not relate just to the physical space, although that does have a part to play, but to symbolic and abstract aspects of HE, and the approach to teaching and learning, particularly in terms of the emphasis and value placed on scholarship and research. Of great significance here is the extent to which teaching staff engage in scholarship and research and the ways in which this is used to inform their professional practice. This can be a particular challenge for HE practitioners who are based in FE settings, since, unlike universities, FE colleges tend not to have a tradition of research. However, staff can engage with research and scholarship by registering for higher degrees and, as part of their professional practice, undertaking Action Research or Practitioner Research. Undertaken in a critical and rigorous manner, such research can usefully inform both individual practice and the wider community. In addition, scholarship and research by practitioners provide opportunities for discussion and debate with students: those discussions themselves then form 'intellectual spaces' which can support students in their own academic development and give them permission to think, explore and question. Virtual intellectual spaces can also support such activities: a discussion thread around specific ideas and concepts provides an easily accessible (especially for part-time students) forum where they have the 'space' to develop their thinking.

Creating intellectual and academic spaces also depends on the organisation promoting the symbolism of HE to create a space where students feel it is safe to explore, think and question. Broadly speaking, the symbolic aspects of HE relate to the broad culture (and ethos!) found within the field (for a discussion on field, see the section on Bourdieu in Chapter 3: *College-based higher education:* the students), and reflected through particular forms of behaviour, language and actions which are imbued with specific meanings as well as through particular values (such as the virtue of scholarship) which are also expressed in behaviour, language and actions. Examples of these might be the expectation (both explicit in module specifications and implicit in forming part of a 'hidden' curriculum) that students engage with scholarship and independent learning, and that they use particular academic conventions in the presentation of their work.

REFLECTIVE TASK

This activity consists of two parts. First, you should make a list of the values that you associate with HE. You may wish to discuss this with a colleague, mentor or peer. Now, reflect on a recent session you have taught and evaluate it carefully, considering how you communicated the values associated with HE to your students. Make notes on how you reflected these in your behaviour, your language and your actions.

Where particular behaviours, language and actions are used and communicated in this way they serve to set HE apart as something that is different and elite, continuing a long tradition which dates back to mediaeval times. Throughout history, HE has been a preserve of the elite and this is reflected in both its culture and in the symbolism associated with it. Perhaps the most potent and obvious example of symbolism is the graduation ceremony. Rooted in almost forgotten mediaeval practices and highly ritualised, it follows a similar dramatic format in every higher education institution. An academic procession follows a symbol of the institution's authority (such as a University mace, which is actually descended from mediaeval weaponry) into a hall, where awards are individually conferred by the Chancellor. Formal academic dress, a requirement of such ceremonies for both graduands and academics, also dates back to the Middle Ages, though in this case it is related to the forms of dress worn by the clergy rather than associated with warfare. Graduation ceremonies serve a number of purposes. They symbolise the value – and virtue – of scholarship, but, perhaps more importantly, they also reflect these ancient traditions and allow new institutions, both colleges and universities, to publicly demonstrate their links to them. They also serve as a public recognition of the scholarship of graduands and acknowledge the continuation of the tradition of learning.

Student engagement, such as that described by Jones (2006) also provides opportunities for creating intellectual and academic spaces. In the context of an HE ethos this concept refers both to learning and to extracurricular activities such as *union activity, participation in (and creation of) societies, and the broader under-graduate social context* (Jones, 2006, page 6). As discussed in the introduction to this chapter, there can be particular practical challenges in facilitating such activity in a college context. However, it is relatively easy to establish student-led activities such as subject reading groups based on the book club principle (which can also operate in virtual space) or debating societies which provide opportunities both for engagement with the wider programme and for creating new and different intellectual spaces. In addition, as Jones goes on to argue, other forms of student engagement, such as representation within formal college structures, allow students to engage with and influence different aspects of their experience and as such *offer the opportunity for students to determine and shape decisions affecting many aspects of participation at the under-graduate level* (Jones, ibid). These forms of wider engagement with the programme serve the twin purposes of contributing to the development of an HE ethos and supporting the college in meeting key audit criteria such as those determined by the QAA or a validating institution.

REFLECTIVE TASK

Creating an HE ethos

Following an electrical fire, six classrooms and the library in the HE Centre in which you teach are severely damaged by smoke and water. As a result your classes have been moved for at least the next term to an under-utilised room in the co-located FE buildings of the college, which are a few minutes walk away. The classroom you have been allocated is located in the Special Needs department of the college, and seats 20 comfortably. It is furnished with 'standard' college tables and chairs. It has a smart board and a whiteboard but no PCs. There are two wall displays, one about managing money and one about sexual health. Thinking about the room itself and other intellectual spaces (such as time for scholarship and virtual spaces), consider the following:

- How could you adapt this room to create an HE ethos in terms of the four-dimensional typography proposed by Jones (2006)?
- How could you make it into an 'intellectual space'?
- How could make it 'feel' like an HE space?

Discuss this with a peer or colleague and write down your ideas: we will return to them at the end of the chapter.

How HE 'feels' different from FE

Another issue with the HE ethos, is that it is not something which can be quantified: to a great extent, an ethos is felt, rather than observed. Therefore, although for the purposes of HEFCE, the QAA and the HEA it is possible to say that the ethos is reflected in certain observable aspects of the programmes offered and in the college surroundings, it can be argued that an ethos is more than this, since the 'feel' will reflect the values and culture within the setting. Secondly, it is likely that the ethos will be different in each institution, irrespective of whether it is a university or a college. This is because an ethos is closely linked to the values associated with particular forms of education and in particular institutions. These can vary widely: in terms of college-based higher education the variations are clearly reflected in the work by Bathmaker et al. (2008) alluded to earlier, and it is acknowledged that each institution will have its own distinctive ethos (HEFCE, 2009, page 1). Despite this, quality audits will look for specific evidence of an HE ethos (such as particular approaches to learning, teaching and assessment or particular types of student engagement with quality enhancement). This was particularly evident in, for example, the old Integrated Quality and Enhancement Review (IQER) conducted by the QAA, and now replaced by the Review of College Higher Education. Further, QA Audits of this type are characteristic of HE and different to those used in FE.

This emphasis on the observable can make it difficult to consider how HE 'feels' and the ways in which this differs from FE. However, the 'feel' is an integral part of the ethos of any setting or organisation, so it is worth trying to unpick the differences, and consider ways in which an HE 'feel' might be promoted. A primary difference in the 'feel' between the two phases might be ascribed to the different motivations students have for undertaking their programmes, which also has implications for the type of learning they undertake. At FE level motivation is largely extrinsic – students will be goal orientated, undertaking programmes as a means to access higher levels of training or education, for example, or because it is a requirement of their employer. In addition, a high proportion of young people accessing FE have had unsuccessful school careers and are, to a greater or lesser extent, disaffected from learning, something which is a significant challenge for practitioners in FE. However, students undertaking HE programmes tend to have much higher levels of intrinsic motivation: as well as factors such as career development, they are motivated by a desire to achieve, and to do something for themselves. This motivation is often related to personal histories and experiences, and is reflected in the lengths students will go to, and the sacrifices they will make, in order to achieve their academic goal: it is also more closely associated with the demands for deep and autonomous learning made by HE.

A second way in which HE 'feels' different to FE focuses on different approaches – and values – placed on teaching and learning. HE values scholarship and intellectually demanding forms of learning. While these values are shared by many practitioners in FE, the process and outcome driven nature of learning and assessment in most vocational programmes, as well as other challenges faced by FE teachers, can make it difficult to promote such values in day-to-day practice. In contrast, the emphasis on independent learning in HE (another way in which it 'feels' different) enables lecturers to demonstrate this value on a day-to-day basis as they encourage students to develop new under-standings and strategies for learning. It also places a different type of expectation on the students, and is reflective of different forms of curriculum to those commonly used in FE. Additionally, HE students are required to adapt to new forms of assessment, as well as learning. In many of the disciplines which are heavily concentrated in colleges, and which are focused on the students' own professional practice, assessments have a reflective element which is drawn on to consider strategies for developing practice. This key characteristic of professional behaviour among learners is another way in which HE differs – and thus has a different 'feel' – to FE. Finally, more collegiate relationships are apparent between students and lecturers in HE, something which recognises the life experiences and understandings of the students, particularly the more mature and those undertaking programmes which involve an element of professional practice.

REFLECTIVE TASK

Refer back to the Reflective Task 'How HE feels different to FE' at the beginning of this chapter. In the light of this section above can you add to your list of differences? Did you come up with any ideas that are specific to your disciplinary area? How could you use your ideas to promote an HE ethos?

HE ethos in practice

So, how do individual colleges promote an HE ethos? According to Mark Hodgkinson, HE Manager at Derby College, the HE ethos is difficult to 'pin down', as it has multiple definitions. However, he believes that there is a distinctive HE in FE ethos, and likened this to differences in ethos between all HE institutions. The features he described are broadly similar to those illustrated in Jones's four-dimensional typology as being charac-teristic of HE in FE. Some of these, he suggests, are easier to promote than others.

The college adopts a modern approach of ensuring that there is a clear distinction between HE and FE within the same college through a range of activities, behaviours and processes, which include:

- *employability activities;*
- *policy and procedures;*
- *terminology;*
- *QA systems aligned with QAA;*
- *infrastructure to support students, e.g. Student Loans contact;*
- *staff development;*
- *programme design to take into account HE QA.*

The approach taken varies from a completely separate approach to integration into FE systems. For example, tutor remission time and timetabling is common across all levels. However, there are some challenges in developing an HE ethos in a college-based context. Appropriate infrastructure helps to promote an HE ethos with the obvious emphasis on a culture of independent study and an active Students Union. The additional opportunities afforded by extra-curricula organisations such as sports and leisure clubs, accommodation areas and bars and social areas all help to create a different atmosphere. These are all extensive in universities and add to the university student culture. In HE in FE generally, however, these are underdeveloped. Another key aspect of the HE infrastructure links to library format and use, such as opening times and other facilities. The college tries to develop the learning resources to support programmes and develop facilities that mirror those of a university, but they are in most cases not yet as extensive, e.g. library opening times. However, HE in FE has particular strengths associated with student support.

A different approach is adopted in HE in FE to take account of the nature of HE. We place greater emphasis on student support; smaller numbers means that we have a more identifiable community of learners and offer greater access to tutors. Both HE and FE develop technical abilities but FE centres are more likely to develop practical approaches. HE in FE does develop independent learning but more slowly, and in most cases there is more contact time to support this.

The HE ethos relates very much to staff as well as students. The university culture includes research and FE does very little pure research, but we do adopt a broad definition of Scholarly Activity. This includes programme development and course delivery development as well as CPD and we also encourage it with project developments, which are both internally and externally funded and generated.

Mark's comments are reflective of the distinctive ethos of college-based higher education, as well as some of the characteristics and activities common across the HE in FE sector. He also illustrates one of its key strengths: support strategies which enable non-traditional learners to develop the independent learning skills they need to succeed, something which the studies cited earlier (Cockburn, 2007; Burkill et al., 2008) have suggested is something which makes college-based higher education both a truly distinctive experience and a positive choice for many students.

Conclusion

There is a macro-level expectation that college-based higher education should successfully promote an HE ethos. However, there is limited research into exactly what this implies for colleges, who rely largely on guidelines produced by national bodies such as HEFCE, the QAA and the HEA. Inevitably, the ethos of any institution is determined to a great extent by the culture and values of the staff team working there, something which can be influenced by disciplinary as well as institutional values and culture. This means that each college with an HE provision will have its own distinct ethos, although all colleges will have some characteristics in common. These are likely to include features such as a degree of separateness for HE students, an expectation that students will engage in more independent forms learning, provision of the resourcing to support this, and involvement of students with broader aspects of the programme such as social groups and quality enhancement processes, as well as symbolic trademarks of HE such as graduation ceremonies.

It is also evident that there is a distinct 'HE in FE' ethos (Cockburn, 2007, page 18, see also the discussion with Mark Hodgkinson), which is something to be valued and which is based on intimate understandings of the needs and motivations of the students who access college-based higher education. Finally, it is also apparent that although the HE ethos can sometimes seem to be an abstract concept of little priority among the heavy daily demands of professional practice, it is important to note that it is critical in the promotion of skills and behaviours such as independent learning and valuing scholarship which support student achievement both at and beyond their level of study. This demonstrates the importance of developing an HE ethos in college-based higher education, and the value of practitioners in the sector exploring ways in which they can promote such an ethos as part of their own professional practice.

A SUMMARY OF **KEY POINTS**

During this chapter we have looked at the following key issues:
- ➢ The development of an HE ethos is regarded as an important aspect of providing HE programmes by organisations such as HEFCE, the QAA and the HEA.
- ➢ An HE ethos encompasses a range of concrete and abstract characteristics, from material aspects such as infrastructure and teaching and learning resources, to the more esoteric, such as the promotion of scholarship.
- ➢ These characteristics vary from institution to institution as they are themselves influenced by factors such as specific institutional and disciplinary values and cultures.
- ➢ Some research has suggested that there is a distinct HE in FE ethos which is different to an HE in HE ethos and is bound up in specific understandings of the needs of students accessing college-based higher education.

Branching options

Reflection

Returning to the Reflective Task, Creating an HE ethos, re-visit the ideas you wrote down. Consider how you might effectively integrate these ideas into your existing professional practice in order to develop such an ethos further. What type of evaluation/ action research might you use to assess their relative success and how might your new understandings inform your professional practice?

Analysis

Much of the emphasis on HE ethos is associated with the intellectual and academic demands of HE programmes, and the different ways in which these are taught. Much of this teaching draws on the scholarship and understanding of the lecturer. How do you develop your own scholarship and practitioner research? How does this inform your professional practice?

Research

There is a paucity of research exploring the value of an HE ethos in college-based higher education and the ways in which it is characterised. How might you use research to develop your understanding of these issues? What specific issues do you think need to be explored?

REFERENCES   REFERENCES   REFERENCES   REFERENCES

Ainley, P. (2008) The varieties of student experience – an open research question and some ways to answer it, *Studies in Higher Education*, 33(5): 615–24.

Bathmaker, A., Brooks, G., Parry, G. and Smith, D. (2008) Dual-sector further and higher education: policies, organisations and students in transition, *Research Papers in Education*, 23 (2):125–37.

Burkill, S., Rodway Dyer, S. and Stone, M. (2008) Lecturing in higher education in further education settings, *Journal of Further and Higher Education*, 32(4): 321–31.

Burns, D. (2007) Conceptualising and Interpreting Organizational Boundaries between Further and Higher Education in 'Dual Sector' Institutions: Where are they and what do they do? Paper presented at the International Conference on Researching Transitions in Lifelong Learning, 22–24 June 2007, at the University of Stirling, UK.

Clancy, P. and Goastellec, G. (2007) Exploring access and equity in higher education: policy and performance in a comparative perspective, *Higher Education Quarterly*, 61: 136–54.

Cockburn, J. (2007) Case Study 1: A Case Study of City College Norwich, in M. Watts, *The Role of the Regional Further Education Colleges in Delivering Higher Education in the East of England*. Association of Universities in the East of England.

Crozier, G., Reay, D., Clayton, J., Colliander, L. and Grinstead, J. (2008) Different strokes for different folks: diverse students in diverse institutions – experiences of higher education, *Research Papers in Education,* 23(2): 167–77.

Gallacher, J. (2006) Blurring the boundaries or creating diversity? The contribution of the further education colleges to higher education in Scotland, *Journal of Further and Higher Education,* 30(1): 43–58.

HEFCE (2009) *Guide for Members of Higher Education Governing Bodies in the UK.* Bristol: HEFCE.

Jones, R. (2006) *A Higher Education Ethos: A review of information and literature relating to the creation of an ethos of higher education in the context of further education.* Higher Education Academy. Available online at: https://www.google.co.uk/url?sa=t&rct=j&q=&esrc=s&source=web&cd=1&ved=0CDEQFjAA&url=http%3A%2F%2Fwww.ics.heacademy.ac.uk%2FHEinFE%2Fdocuments%2FA_Higher_Education_Ethos.doc&ei=6xr0UOfoFLCp0AWdmoD4AQ&usg=AFQjCNE2JljgCXEqB26F3fk4Ut5X-HyVNg&sig2=0wq9mXK_LFWFCYoPaX3a6g&bvm=bv.1357700187,d.d2k&cad=rjt (accessed 03/06/13).

King, M., Buckland, M., Greenwood, M., Ives, S. and Thompson, A. (2010) *Strategic Options, Operational Challenges: A Study of Higher Education Delivered in a Further Education Setting.* Coventry: Mixed Economy Group/LSIS.

Moreau, M-P. and Leathwood, C. (2006) Balancing paid work and studies: working (class) students in higher education, *Studies in Higher Education,* 31(1): 23–42.

Quality Assurance Agency (2013) *QAA Homepage.* Available online at: www.qaa.ac.uk/Pages/default.aspx (accessed 03/06/13).

Weatherald, C and Moseley, R. (2003) Higher Education in Further Education Colleges: Researching and developing good practice. Paper presented to the 2003 FACE Conference. Available online at: www.face.stir.ac.uk/Weatheraldp52.htm (accessed 03/06/13).

3

College-based higher education:
the students

By the end of this chapter you will be able to:

- understand the particular needs and characteristics of students who choose to undertake college-based higher education;
- be able to contextualise these within the context of theoretical ideas on structure and agency;
- understand some of the differences between traditional and non-traditional students and the settings they choose to study in.

Introduction

It is apparent that there are significant differences in the type of students who access college-based higher education, when compared with those who access university-based higher education. For example, a majority of students at university are young undergraduates who have progressed from school or college straight to university at around the age of 18. In comparison, many of the HE students in FE colleges are mature people, often seeking to either develop their career or to make a career change. It is also apparent that there are differences in terms of the social class background of people who access HE in colleges when compared to those who go directly to university. So, how do we know this and what are the reasons for it? In order to discuss this, we will draw on concepts developed by Pierre Bourdieu, a French sociologist, and on the theories of Phil Hodkinson, a British academic who has undertaken extensive research into transitions through education to work. We will illustrate these ideas through the use of profiles of students we have known or taught.

Bourdieu's theories use the terms habitus, field, structure and agency. He uses *habitus* and *field* to explain his theories of *structure* and *agency*. The term habitus is used to explain the ways in which individuals think and behave.

According to Bourdieu, the ways in which we think and behave are related to our primary knowledge of life and situation and to what Robbins (1998, page 35) describes as the *inheritance of the accumulated experiences of [our] antecedents*. In other words, to the culture, values, beliefs and social practices we are brought up with. Bourdieu explains these practices as a game, which takes place in a 'field'. A field is a structure, organisation or group in which particular social and cultural practices are expressed through specific language and behaviour, which is often is confusing or alien to outsiders. Examples of fields might include social class, education, hairdressing or the armed forces.

BEEFECIIXE IVSK
REFLECTIVE TASK

With a group of colleagues or fellow students, think about your specialist area and jot down any behaviour or language that you can think of which is specific to that professional area. Much of the language you think of might be acronyms. For example, the acronym *ILP* has a meaning specific to education but would be confusing to an outsider. Similarly, the term *care planning* has a particular meaning in Health and Social Care, which would be unclear to most people outside that vocational area.

When you have finished, compare your list with that of a peer or colleague from a different professional area. How confusing do you find each other's lists? What does this tell you about the relative ease or difficulty students may have in progressing to HE (a field of its own) and becoming part of a specific occupational, academic or vocational group (another field)?

Structure and agency

Structure relates to social structures that control or influence the lives of individuals. Examples of structures would be social class, the family, education and the state; however, the concept may also be used to describe *embodied* structures. These arise from characteristics such as race, disability and gender, which can determine and reproduce how people think and behave. For example, a young female and a young male are likely to have very different (gender-specific) ideas about the types of job that might be right for them. Agency may be defined as the ability that agents or individuals have to control their own actions or destiny within those structures. This means that the field *orients choices* (Bourdieu, 1990, page 66), but individual agency will determine which of those choices are made and this will in turn be influenced by the habitus of the individual, their motivation and values.

Student profiles in college-based higher education

So, what do these theories and concepts tell us, and how do they help us to understand our students? The ideas were used extensively by Phil Hodkinson and colleagues during the 1980s, as they studied young people through their school to work trajectory, a time which is critical in terms of *career decision making* (Hodkinson et al., 1996, page 146; Hodkinson, 1998, page 126). Although the focus of this study was on young people, the findings can be applied more broadly, and have particular significance for those professionals involved in supporting HE students in college contexts.

In trying to explain how and why young people make particular choices in terms of work and education Hodkinson et al. (1996, pages 146–7) argued that lifestyle and habitus are inseparable and interrelated, constrained and enabled by the social and cultural conditions within which people live. In turn, these are influenced by the actions of that individual. They also develop the notion of Horizons for Action, originally proposed by Hodkinson and Sparkes in 1993, which suggests that career choices are also constrained and enabled, in this case by external opportunities and personal subjective perceptions (1996, page 3). Put simply, this means that people make 'pragmatic' career choices based on what is available to them in the local economy (Hodkinson et al., 1996; Ball et al., 2000; Bloomer and Hodkinson, 2000; Hodkinson and Bloomer, 2001) as well as based on what they think is a suitable job for them, something which will be influenced by social class and gender (Hodkinson, 1996, page 148). This helps to explain the gendered nature of most vocational subjects, such as construction, childcare, beauty therapy and engineering – most people incline towards programmes that they perceive to be gender appropriate.

Therefore, each individual will have a personal idea of what sort of job they can do, influenced by gendered beliefs and the values and culture they have been brought up with. They will also be constrained in their choices by what is available to them, perhaps locally, or perhaps in terms of what they are able to access in the light of the credentials they gained at school. Personal views and beliefs of 'what is right for me' will also extend to education, and this is particularly important where students come from families with no history of accessing higher (or sometimes even further) education as it might influence or limit their own aspirations, but may also be the focus of conflict between themselves and friends and family. This is illustrated in the following Case Study and Reflective Task.

CASE STUDY

Donna was born and brought up on a large social housing estate in a disadvantaged part of a large northern city. She disliked school, where she was bullied, and left at 16 with no qualifications. She did a variety of low pay, low skill work before marrying at the age of 20. She went on to have three children but had to return to work when she was 33 after her husband left her. She found work as a care assistant at a nursing home close to where she lived. Donna loved her work and found that she had a great affinity with elderly people. Her employer supported her to do a mandatory level 2 NVQ and two years later, a level 3. Despite this, Donna recognised that her career options were limited. She explored entry requirements for nursing but found that she did not meet them. Undeterred, she applied for a place on a BTEC HNC level 4 in Health and Social Care at her local college.

She chose her programme because, subject to certain conditions, it offered a guaranteed place on a nursing degree programme at a local university. In order to meet those conditions, during the first year of this course she also did a GCSE in maths and during her second year, a GCSE in English. All these programmes were undertaken part-time, fitting around her 12-hour day and night shifts in the nursing home and her domestic responsibilities. She became ill during her second year, possibly due to the pressure of work, childcare and study, and considered giving up when she could not pay the final instalment of her fees. This coincided with the breakdown of her relationship with her boyfriend who did not see the point of going to college. Donna's pastoral tutor offered a shoulder to cry on and liaised with Student Support and the college finance department. With this help, Donna finally gained her qualification – and a place on a degree programme – at the age of 42.

REFLECTIVE TASK

Reflect on Donna's story in the context of Hodkinson's ideas around career decision-making and Horizons for Action and discuss your ideas with a colleague or fellow student. How is Donna constrained socially, culturally and financially during her career? How is she enabled? What influence might social class and gender have had on her career and education choices?

If we accept that college-based higher education is, like all other forms of education, class specific, then we have to accept that the profiles of students accessing these forms of HE will, similarly to Donna, reflect a particular social class demographic. Therefore, most, if not all, of the students who access college-based higher education will come from partic-ular socio-economic groups that might be described as working class. They will also have other similar characteristics, which Cockburn (2006, page 19) has defined as:

- *older and returning to study;*
- *studying part-time;*
- *living locally and with their family (whether with or as parents);*
- *being in employment and being career-focused;*
- *not looking for a lifestyle change;*
- *studying vocational rather than more 'academic' programmes; and/or*
- *sensitive to financial matters.*

He goes on to argue that *the variance within the HE in FE learner profile is significant against virtually every measurable factor compared to the typical university cohort* (ibid).

It is important to think about student *identities* at this point. Identity is a complex concept, which refers to the whole of the individual personality we develop over time. It is bound up in all our formative experiences, including the social and cultural background we come from, our work, social and educational experiences as well as personal values and beliefs. Education can make a significant difference to identity. Where it is vocational, students move through a process of 'becoming' (Colley, 2006) as they adopt the understandings, language and professional attributes of particular occupations.

All education, both vocational and academic, also confers what Bourdieu and Passeron (1990) refer to as cultural capital. *Cultural capital* refers to forms of different knowledge (for example, social and intellectual), which are acquired over time and have value in society in relation to status and power. The term was coined by Bourdieu and Passeron to try to explain the differ-ent educational outcomes of young people from different social classes. They believed that where parents can confer cultural capital on their children, because they themselves have had access to education, the children will achieve more educationally than those with more limited access to cultural capital (e.g. those with uneducated parents and/or from more disadvantaged backgrounds). However, there are risks associated with being the first generation of a family to pursue HE and with the acquisition of cultural capital that HE brings. For example, a student may become more questioning as a result of their education, form opinions which are at vari-ance with those of family and friends, or become open to new experiences which are different to those they associate with family and friends. In a nutshell, education tends to make people more 'middle class' in their values, attitudes and approach to life, something that can result in tension between them and their families and friends. In a similar vein, Michael Watts (2006, pages 309–10) has argued that moving to HE requires *disproportionate sacrifices* from disad-vantaged young people, as those from groups who have traditionally been excluded from HE will have to *adapt and change in order to fit in*. Pursuing college-based higher education, for many people, might be one way of avoiding the need to adapt and change quite so much.

Student backgrounds

A key characteristic of many students pursuing HE in college is that they are drawn from the local community. Unlike universities, who have a national pool to draw from, college-based HE draws almost all its students from the local area. Much more than universities, FE colleges are strongly located in local communities, often with close links to local industry and they offer the local opportunities that are so important for their students. Thus, the college is part of the community, drawing its students from the community and returning them to work within the same community. This sense of localism and the strength of the relationship with the local community is a key factor both in the programmes students choose to undertake (often informed by local job opportunities) and in the strength of individual student relationships with the college.

This does highlight one of the key differences between HE in universities and that in colleges: although some universities do have a strong local demographic, they still draw many students from a national pool. Colleges, on the other hand, do not. Other differences include the almost entirely vocational nature of the 'HE in FE' curriculum and the tendency of many HE college students to fall into the non-traditional, or widening participation, cohort.

This reflects the fact that HE, as in other phases, is *class specific*. This means that certain institutions or forms of HE will draw most of their students from particular social classes or *class fractions*. This is reflected across the HE sector, which may be seen as a spectrum, with the most selective, high status universities drawing the most privileged students at one end, and the least selective, lowest status institutions drawing the most disadvantaged students at the other.

Typically, therefore, universities such as Oxford and Cambridge, as well as those which form part of the Russell Group, draw significant numbers of students from relatively affluent backgrounds who have been educated in the independent sector, grammar schools and 'good' comprehensive schools achieving A levels with high grades (A*–B). These universities tend to focus on 'academic' subjects (such as English, History or Maths) and elite vocational and professional degrees such as Law, Medicine and some forms of Engineering. Across the spectrum, less elite HE providers tend to offer a wider range of less elite vocational programmes and a narrower range of 'academic' subjects. They also take more young people with lower alternative entry qualifications who have, themselves, gained these at less prestigious institutions (possibly forming part of the widening participation cohort discussed in Chapter 1).

This is not to say that elite institutions take only middle-class young people, or that FE colleges offering HE programmes take only the most disadvantaged. However, it does mean that this is broadly the case, and the very fact that the education system is structured in this way creates more barriers to overcome for those who are most disadvantaged in educational terms which can impact not only on the type of HE they are able to access, but on their life and career chances far into the future. That said, for most students undertaking HE in college, this has been a positive decision based on factors such as familiarity with the college, location, and the ability to study part-time away from a setting which primarily consists of young undergraduates.

The following case studies and learning activities are reflective of some of the reasons students choose college-based higher education, and their potential implications.

CASE STUDY

1: Jo

Jo lives in a small town in the rural midlands of England. She left school at 16 with a few GCSEs. These included English at grade C and Maths at grade D. She did a variety of jobs, mainly in retail, until she had her daughter, Chloe, when she was 19. Jo was keen to be involved in Chloe's education and helped out first at nursery, then at school. When Chloe was six, Jo was employed by the primary school as a midday supervisor, and eventually, two years later, as a teaching assistant. With the support of the school, Jo completed an NVQ level 2, and then an NVQ level 3. By the time Chloe was 11, Jo had decided to enrol on a foundation degree in Education Studies at her local college, with a long-term aim of progressing to an honours degree and subsequently a PGCE or GTP (Graduate Teacher Programme). A top-up to BA (Hons) is available at the college and at a local university, which is a half hour drive away. The same university also offers a PGCE primary.

2: Phoebe

Phoebe is also from a small town in the rural midlands. She had always wanted to be a primary teacher. She did work experience at a local primary school while in the sixth form and helped out with cubs and brownies. She took 9 GCSEs, achieving all A and B grades, then took A levels in English, History and Art. She progressed to an 'old' university in the south of England, where she did a history degree. After this, she progressed to a primary PGCE at the same university.

Activity

In small groups, compare these two case studies and discuss the following:

- **To what extent is Jo's background typical of your own students? To what extent is it different?**
- **To what extent is Phoebe's background typical of your own students? To what extent is it different?**
- **In which ways is social class a factor in these differences and similarities?**
- **What specific challenges might Jo face in terms of completing her education and getting a job, which could disadvantage her in comparison to Phoebe?**
- **Does Jo have anything in her background that might confer advantages that Phoebe does not have?**
- **How do your ideas relate to the theoretical notion of lifestyle and career being 'constrained and enabled' by the social and cultural conditions within which Jo and Phoebe live?**

Barriers to participation in HE in FE

As the discussion throughout this chapter has suggested, personal values and attitudes towards education, related to habitus and derived from an individual's upbringing and background, are highly significant in determining whether they will eventually access HE. For example, a person from a family with no history or experience of HE may well regard it as something for other people, who are different to them, perhaps reflecting an understanding of the potential need to 'adapt and change' mentioned earlier. Some individuals associate HE with affluence and social status, excluding themselves on the basis of social class. Although colleges have drawn significant numbers of students to HE programmes because they are perceived by many students to be a more familiar and less threatening environment than a university, the HE centres many institutions have established, partly to promote an 'HE ethos' (see Chapter 2) may be a double-edged sword. By this, we mean that a move from a familiar and safe college setting to an HE centre may generate similar anxieties and fear of the unknown to those associated with enrolling at university.

A further barrier to participation may be that the programme an individual wishes to pursue is not available at their local college or is not accessible in terms of the times at which it is delivered. Despite the significant expansion in HE programmes in the FE sector (as discussed in Chapter 1), they are still limited in comparison to those available at universities, reflecting the difference in the key focus of the different types of institution. If the wish to pursue a particular programme cannot be met by a local institution, many potential students, particularly those constrained by family responsibilities, may be unable to pursue their education further. Similarly, many people working irregular hours or with caring or childcare responsibilities may have difficulties in accessing a programme which is at a fixed time each week, for example.

Perhaps the most significant barrier to access is the financial cost. Travelling to college, perhaps taking time off work or paying for childcare are not insignificant costs, particularly if a student is in low paid work or in receipt of benefits and these issues alone may create insurmountable barriers to college-based higher education for many students. In addition to these ongoing costs, however, is the issue of fees. Of course, this issue does not just apply to college-based higher education, but is a significant issue across the board since the recent changes to the university fees structure. Despite the fact that HE programmes in colleges tend to be significantly less expensive than those based in universities (broadly speaking, they are around a third cheaper, depending on programme and locality) and that the maximum any institution can charge is (at the time of writing) £9,000, it is this figure that has entered public consciousness. There is emerging anecdotal evidence, which suggests that many potential students do not understand that the fees do not have to be repaid until they are in receipt of an income above £21,000 per annum (2012 figures). Therefore, a confused perception of the likely cost and a lack of understanding of the system for borrowing and repaying the fees may be a factor in some students choosing not to enter HE programmes. However, another issue in relation to this is associated with perceptions of debt. Many young people, having grown up at a time of freely available credit, and familiar with the concept of a student loan, are blasé about the prospect of debt but the same cannot be said about more mature students who make up a significant majority of those accessing college-based higher education. For older students, who possibly have different cultural attitudes to debt, who may have experienced debt and who are likely to have families to support, the very idea of owing thousands of pounds – however it is rationalised – can be problematic, particularly if they have previously had experience of dealing with, for example, solicitors' letters, bailiffs or loan sharks.

REFLECTIVE TASK

Refer back to the case studies of Jo and Phoebe and think about the following:

- What barriers does Jo face in completing her education?
- What barriers does Phoebe face?
- How can your professional practice facilitate students like Jo to overcome the barriers to participation they face?
- Make some notes on this and think of ways in which your ideas could be integrated into your ongoing continuing personal and professional (CPPD) plan.

Subject areas

The recent Lingfield Report (BIS, 2012, page 2) identifies five main aims and associated segments of FE, which include both vocational education (teaching occupational skills) and HE studies. This is important, because the HE programmes that we find being offered in FE colleges are vocational in nature, often building on earlier studies which have prepared students for entry to particular occupations. These HE programmes fall into three broad categories. The first category includes those programmes which lead to professional qualifications such as the level 6 ILEX law and practice higher diploma for students wanting to qualify as a chartered legal executive or solicitor. The second category includes courses which offer qualifications to support more senior roles in specific occupational areas such as foundation degree in construction, which might support advancement to a site manager role and, in the final category, are programmes which enable students to meet minimum academic requirements for entry to professional training. An example of this would be a BA degree in childhood studies, which could then enable the student to access a PGCE programme and qualify as a teacher. It is important also to note that much college-based higher education supports progression through different job roles in particular occupational areas. Many of those taking a BA degree in childhood studies for example, will have been working as teaching assistants and may earlier have undertaken NVQ qualifications and subsequently foundation degrees to support this role. An honours degree and move into teaching would be a planned progression route for many of these students.

REFLECTIVE TASK

Think about the programmes that you teach on. Which broad subject category do they fall into? To what extent are the programmes 'gendered'? What similarities are there in the socio-economic profile of the students?

Discuss your ideas with a mentor or fellow students. To what extent would your responses differ if you taught in a different subject area? What commonalities would there be?

Many of the programmes offered as college-based higher education are also in subject areas that are extremely popular. This can simply be because a particular college offers programmes that are relevant to specific local industry and the skills demands this generates. However, in some cases programmes can be perceived to have particular social and academic status (such as education for example) or, in others, because as well as being perceived to carry particular status they are also considered glamorous (such as fashion design). The subjects offered may also be influenced by relationships with the HEIs and professional bodies that validate many of these qualifications, as well as by individual colleges having long-standing reputations for excellence in specific subject areas.

Admissions routes

The admissions routes to college-based higher education are, in many respects, more complicated than those for universities, something which is related to the progression routes followed by so many students who access this form of HE. Every year, the vast majority of HE applications are drawn from young people applying for undergraduate degree programmes via the UCAS system. This application system is also now used for full-time college-based programmes. However, many students will make direct applications for part-time courses and many of these will already be known to the institution simply because many students remain with the same local organisation throughout their post-school education career. This is particularly the case where students are following particular progression routes – perhaps from a level 3 occupational qualification in further education, to a foundation degree in higher education and subsequently to a 'top-up' programme which leads to an honours degree.

Another admission route commonly used in college-based higher education is Accreditation of Prior Experience and Learning, or APEL. Although subject to rigorous evidence requirements, particularly where APEL is used to access university-validated provision, it is widely used, especially where applicants may have limited educational credentials, but many years of occupational experience in the area they wish to study. Many APEL routes require the submission of evidence of specific levels of ability in, for example, written English as well as evidence of occupational experience and competence. A good example of this is teacher training programmes where it is common for students to claim APEL for the PTLLS preliminary award. However, if this has been awarded at level 3 applicants will be required to complete additional work (in this case, often reflective writing) to demonstrate that they are working at level 4 or above, since level 3 credentials do not attract credit points in HE. Another common means of demonstrating APEL is the use of a portfolio, which will normally be assessed against specific criteria and a pre-determined number of credit points awarded to the applicant who will then complete only part of a programme.

Some students may also use national credit transfer processes, which allow students to move between institutions, taking a transcript of credit achieved with them, and completing their studies at a different institution. While this appears straightforward, difficulties can arise, particularly where programmes are written to comply with external standards or specifications, as in teacher training. Even though two institutions may offer two almost identical programmes based on the same standards, if the time frame for delivery is different, or the numbers of credits awarded to different parts of the programme are not identical, this can create complexities in direct transfer to another programme. In addition, institutions may have regulations about how much credit can be transferred and to what type of programme. Half a foundation degree in fashion design would not, for example, mean that a student could successfully complete the second half of a foundation degree in computer science.

Conclusion

This chapter has explored the profile and background of the 'typical' student undertaking HE in a college context. While all people are individuals, and it is important not to assume that every member of a particular group necessarily shares identical characteristics, it can be helpful to understand our students in terms of their lives and motivations. In doing this, we necessarily have to consider the broad similarities between members of a particular group.

It is apparent that not only do students who study HE in colleges tend to share a range of characteristics but that *the variance within the HE in FE learner profile is significant against virtually every measurable factor compared to the typical university cohort* (Cockburn, 2006, page 19). The characteristics broadly shared by these non-traditional students mean that they often experience a range of barriers to HE, which are significantly greater than those of the average 18-year-old undergraduate. Key factors here are the financial and personal responsibilities associated with being a mature student:

juggling these with studying can prove to be a significant challenge and supporting students to overcome such difficulties often forms a major aspect of the pastoral support which is a major strength of much of the teaching in FE colleges.

The need for pastoral as well as practical support is often recognised by students, and can be a factor in their decision to study at college, rather than university. Not only is the ethos more nurturing than at university, but the HE curriculum in colleges tends to be more highly structured, and this can lead to a perception among students that it is more readily accessible and thus give them greater confidence in pursuing their studies (see Chapter 2 for a more extended discussion).

The particular characteristics of the typical student who pursues HE in a college context can be described as 'constraining and enabling' factors in terms of research around structure and agency and Horizons for Action. The very fact that someone is older, with more personal responsibilities, can constrain their potential for agency and have a significant influence on if, and how, they pursue HE. Conversely, an older student with greater life experience might have been enabled to make much more informed career and education choices than a young person who is still at school and who has no real experience of the world of work.

A SUMMARY OF KEY POINTS

During this chapter we have looked at the following key issues:

➢ Students studying college-based higher education tend to be older, part-time, local and living with their family, employed, not looking for a lifestyle change, studying vocational rather than academic programmes, career focused and sensitive to financial matters (Cockburn, 2006, page 19)

➢ Students studying college-based higher education also tend to fit a particular socio-economic demographic and often come from families with little or no previous experience of HE.

➢ A number of different theoretical ideas suggest that individuals' lives, with particular reference to education and work, are 'constrained and enabled' by their lifestyle and habitus (background) and by the social and cultural conditions in which they live.

➢ College-based higher education offers a wide range of access routes to an increasing variety of largely vocational programmes which provide opportunities for career development and progression.

Students accessing college-based higher education do share many important characteristics. However, they are also very different in many important ways. Each one is an individual, striving to make the best future they can for themselves and their family and making the best choices and decisions they can in the context of their individual lives and circumstances. It is these differences, rather than their similarities to others, which inform their individual motivations for being in HE, and it also these differences that will dictate the type of pastoral support they will need to ensure that they become one of the many success stories of college-based higher education.

Branching options

Reflection

As you look back over this chapter, reflect on the ways in which you think of your students. Has this changed? Have you developed different understandings of your students and their life and learning experiences? Talk with colleagues at work or with other students and compare your views. How might this help to inform your professional practice?

Analysis

At the beginning of this chapter you were asked to discuss Donna's story in the context of Hodkinson's ideas of Horizons for Action and career decision-making. Revisit the questions, and relate them to two of your own students. What does this tell you about those students? How can this understanding inform your professional practice?

Research

Much of the research which has been undertaken into HE has focused on the in/equalities which are derived from societal structures which constrain individuals' potential for agency and thus impact on students' opportunities. Explore some of the literature listed under References. How does this relate to your students? How might it inform your practitioner research and professional practice?

REFERENCES   REFERENCES   REFERENCES   REFERENCES

Ball, S.J., Maguire, M. and Macrae, S. (2000) *Choice, Pathways and Transitions Post-16 New Youth, New Economies in the Global City*. London: Routledge/Falmer.

Bloomer, M. and Hodkinson, P. (2000) Learning careers: continuity and change in young people's dispositions to learning, *British Educational Research Journal*, 26(5): 583–97.

Bourdieu, P. (1990) *The Logic of Practice*. Cambridge: Polity Press.

Bourdieu, P. and Passeron, J-C. (1990) *Reproduction in Education, Society and Culture* (2nd edition). London: Sage.

Cockburn, J (2006) Case Study 1: A Case Study of City College Norwich, in M. Watts, *The Role of the Regional Further Education Colleges in Delivering Higher Education in the East of England*. Association of Universities in the East of England. Full Report available at: www.theresearchcentre.co.uk/files/docs/publications/he0005.pdf (accessed 20/12/2012).

Colley, H. (2006) Learning to labour with feeling: class, gender and emotion in childcare education and training, *Contemporary Issues in Early Childhood*, 7(1): 15–29.

Department for Business, Innovation and Skills (BIS) (2012) *Professionalism in Further Education* (The Lingfield Report). London: The Stationery Office.

Hodkinson, P. (1996) Careership: The Individual, Choices and Markets in the Transition to Work, in J. Avis, M. Bloomer, G. Esland, D. Gleeson and P. Hodkinson, *Knowledge and Nationhood*. London: Cassell.

Hodkinson, P. (1998) Career Decision Making and the Transition from School to Work, in M. Grenfell and D. James (eds) *Bourdieu and Education: Acts of Practical Theory*. London: Falmer Press.

Hodkinson, P. and Bloomer, M. (2001) Dropping out of further education: complex causes and simplistic policy assumptions, *Research Papers in Education*, 16(2): 117–40. Available online at: www.ingentaconnect.com/content/routledg/rred;jsessionid=4btlk1qi4s9q3.alice (accessed 03/06/13).

Hodkinson, P. and Sparkes, A. (1993) Young people's career choices and careers guidance action planning: A case-study of training credits in action, *British Journal of Guidance & Counselling*, 21(3): 246–61. Available online at: www.informaworld.com/smpp/title~content=t713406946~db=all~tab=issueslist~branches=21 - v21 (accessed 03/06/13).

Hodkinson, P., Sparkes, A. and Hodkinson, H. (1996) *Triumphs and Tears: Young People, Markets and the Transition from School to Work*. London: David Fulton.

Robbins, D. (1998) The Need for an Epistemological Break, in M. Grenfell and D. James (eds) *Bourdieu and Education: Acts of Practical Theory*. London: Falmer Press.

Watts, M. (2006) Disproportionate sacrifices: Ricoeur's theories of justice and the widening participation agenda for higher education in the UK, *Journal of Philosophy of Education*, 40(3): 301–12.

4

Planning and preparing for teaching HE in FE

By the end of this chapter you will be able to:

- critically evaluate key concepts in planning and preparing for teaching on HE courses;
- understand how module and programme specifications are written in HE and how these shape teaching;
- apply a range of key concepts to the development of HE courses.

Designing a higher education course

In this chapter we will look at a number of the technical elements involved in course or programme design and we will discuss the writing of the documentation associated with this design. The process of course design in HE is not, however, wholly or even principally technical. To pose the question, 'what do you want your students to learn?' is also to pose the question, 'what are your values?'. Elliott Eisner, an important figure in the research of curriculum design, talked about 'curriculum ideologies' which are sets of values that determine decisions over what a course should contain or do. Some course writers may be able to identify, articulate and justify their own values, but many others are simply not aware of what they take for granted in their planning. What an IT student should learn in the first year of a higher national diploma is, for some, self-evident; a tutor may say, 'I know the workplace and this is what the workplace needs' or 'that is the way you teach electrical engineering', perhaps. These tacit beliefs, however benign, are unexamined and so are not open to challenge. They are not even perceived as decisions because, as Susan Toohey (1999, page 44) puts it, *alternative views are literally 'unthinkable'*. A walk around many large educational institutions will provide a physical manifestation of these tacit beliefs in the ways that learning spaces are set out: lecture theatres with raked seating, classrooms with tables and chairs in rows or labs with computers in a line along the walls may derive from a view of education that is individualised and didactic. Elsewhere, there may be tables and chairs set out in groups or workshops with large benches to allow collaboration, suggesting a view of education as a social activity. Similarly, the form of assessment within a course is also highly susceptible to what is taken for granted even if, once again, it is just the emphasis on individual achievement not cooperation. This is not to suggest that any of these beliefs are necessarily wrong. Rather, this is to encourage those who are designing courses to reflect on and to problematise their decisions in order to enhance their courses and to develop themselves as professionals. Reflective practice means examining our decisions, not seeking ways to justify them once they are made.

Of course, HE courses can teach much more than what is set out in the syllabus content or programme document. This is especially relevant to professional attitudes and ethos on vocational courses, but it applies elsewhere. A chemist may demonstrate laboratory protocols in how she behaves while teaching, just as a teacher educator may model good practice (or even bad practice for that matter) in his approach to trainee teachers.

REFLECTIVE TASK

Think about your own teaching practice and what you prioritise when assessing students to consider these questions. Discussions with colleagues who have observed your teaching may help you with this task. How does your practice derive from what you believe is important in your subject and in education more generally? If someone were to observe you teaching, what might they say about your values? How would they recognise your values in your practice? How would you articulate your own educational values? From where do they come, your own education, for example? Finally, how do these values shape your decisions in curriculum design?

The course design process as set out in some textbooks will start logically with the establishment of demand through rigorous needs analysis or market research. There will then be a structured sifting of approaches and content before a syllabus and scheme of work emerge as a final logical step of a rigorous and measured process. New courses, however, often start out with the enthusiasm of a tutor or manager who wants to try something out and has the energy to see the process through. Nonetheless, some structure will help the process of course design and is indispensable for the process of institutional validation. This process is discussed more fully below and in Chapter 9. Essentially, this is when the awarding body or institution verifies the quality of potential courses before allowing them to run.

Here are some questions to ask at the very start of designing a course. You are likely to be asked these or similar during any validation.

- What evidence is there of demand for the course?
- How will the course be funded?
- Will the course require HEFCE numbers?
- Are there sufficient qualified tutors to run the course?
- Are there sufficient resources such as specialist equipment and library books for the course?
- Have you allowed sufficient time to write the course and gain validation from the associated awarding body or organisation, especially given that HEIs move rather more slowly than most FE colleges when instigating new provision?
- For vocational or professional provision, does your course meet current standards or requirements?
- Is there a progression route on to the course from your own or local educational organisations?
- Might students who can claim accreditation for prior experience or learning (APEL) join the course? If so, is there a clear procedure for them to follow?

Within the technical and administrative demands that institutions place on those designing courses it can be easy to lose sight of the students and how they will experience courses. Nevertheless, a strong course as well as good course documentation will place students at the centre of any description and rationale. HE in FE students may be especially anxious about the processes involved in starting a course if they have had a long break from education. While we should not let emotional responses to the curriculum infantilise our students, we should carefully think about their probable response to the course and its structure. Similarly, as the questions above indicate, we should think about from where they might have progressed to the course and to where they might progress after the course. For vocational courses that may mean talking to local employers about professional development or career opportunities they need and offer. For all HE courses, however, it means having a clear rationale for how students will benefit from the time and expense they will invest in your course.

REFLECTIVE TASK

Take a course to which you already contribute. What is the rationale for the course to run? How would you persuade a potential student that it was worth the time, commitment and cost of coming on to your course? Your response to that may be instrumental: for example, graduates earn more money; but you should also consider personal development. How would you like your students to be or to think differently once they have completed your course? Finally, where can the students progress once they finish the course, if they choose?

RESEARCH FOCUS

There has been a significant debate around curriculum design and how it relates to knowledge. Michael Young (2008, page 81) states that, *the acquisition of knowledge is the key feature that distinguishes education, whether general, further, vocational or higher, from all other activities*. He argues that curricula need to be based around a body of knowledge and approvingly quotes (ibid, page 83) Judith Williams who wrote:

> *Whether in astrophysics or literature, there is a body of knowledge to be learned and renewed. Most would like [it] to be useful and many would like it to be easy. However, it is not often the former and rarely the latter. What really matters about knowledge is that it is true or rather that we can learn or find the truth or truths as best we can, in any field. This is what education and, more specifically, universities are for.*

Young (ibid, page 89) argues against what might be called skills-based teaching with its emphasis on experiential learning, which is necessarily restricted: *The curriculum cannot be based on everyday practical experience*. Such a curriculum would only recycle that experience. Getting students to think carefully about their experience in a structured way is certainly useful in developing their knowledge but if that experience is limited then so too will the thinking be. So, designing a curriculum or planning for teaching requires clarity about the body of knowledge that you want your students to engage with and learn.

Making sense of modules and programmes

There is a rising expectation of openness and accountability in HE that is apparent, for example, in the importance of the National Student Survey (this is discussed in full in Chapter 9). As part of this general move in the HE sector, programme or course documents are expected to be both accessible to students and, consequently, comprehensible to students. There is some way to go with the latter, however, as there is even discrepancy between the use of the word 'course' or 'programme' to describe a coherent study path leading to a qualification. In this chapter, therefore, we will use the terms interchangeably. Elsewhere, too, the language used in HE module and programme documents is occasionally obscure, as are concepts like the notional study hours and equivalent word counts. This chapter will examine the format and requirements of module and programme documents to help you to both understand and create them. We will start with a brief glossary of some of the terms we use in this chapter which are employed in the design of teaching and learning in HE.

Module or unit

A module or unit is a discrete element of a course with its own learning outcomes and assessment criteria that relate to its credit level (see below). Modules may be compulsory or optional on a course and modules may be shared between courses. This means that students taking a degree in childhood studies and another taking a degree in primary education may both take the same module on children and literacy, for example.

Learning outcomes

These are statements of what the student is expected to have learned after completion of a programme or course. They are very often divided between first, knowledge and understanding and second, abilities. The language used in learning outcomes will reflect the credit level (see below).

Credit and credits

Academic credit exists at various levels in HE and is awarded to a learner in recognition of the achievement of designated learning outcomes at a specified level. A full honours degree will normally have a total of 360 credits, usually divided into 120 credits at Foundation Level (also called level 4 and equivalent to the first year of a full-time three-year degree), 120 credits at Intermediate Level (also called level 5 and equivalent to the second year of a three-year degree) and 120 credits at Honours Level (also called level 6 and equivalent to the third year of a full-time three-year degree). Modules and courses will normally have a set number of credits that correspond to the breadth and intellectual demand of learning required. This combination of credits and credit level is known as *credit value.* A learner accumulates credits towards the total credit required for a programme of study and a qualification such as an MSc, which normally has 180 credits at master's level. The award of credits at a specified level allows courses and modules to be compared within and between colleges and universities. Most HE institutions in the UK use credit in this way and are part of the Credit Accumulation and Transfer System (CATS). Credit can, therefore, be a tool to compare learning achieved in different contexts and it can provide a basis for recognising learning achieved in other institutions. This allows *credit transfer* where a student might 'carry' credits awarded at one institution to put towards the achievement of an award at a second institution.

Intended learning outcomes

These are statements of what students will know after engaging with the module or with the programme and they are expressed from the learners' perspective (learners will know ... and be able to do...). These outcomes should connect directly to the assessment criteria.

Notional study hours

The number of notional study hours of learning on a module is based on how long it should take a typical student to achieve the learning outcomes that are specified for the module or programme. This total number will include formal classes as well as an estimate of the amount of time the student will spend in preparation for these classes, along with independent study, plus revision and the completion of coursework required on the module. Notional hours are directly linked to credits in the UK; one credit represents 10 notional hours of learning. This helps institutions to set the credit value of a module or programme. For example, a module that is estimated to involve 150 notional hours of learning will be assigned 15 credits and one that involves 300 notional hours of learning will be assigned 30 credits. Remember, the number of hours is only notional. That is, the total is a best judgement based on an average student and is only meant as a guide for students and tutors. Therefore a student may take a shorter or longer time to complete the module but still receive the same credits.

Programme specification documents

Programme specification documents (PSDs) were introduced so that potential students could find clear descriptions of HE courses in order to be able to compare these courses before deciding which was most appropriate for their purposes. They are meant to inform the potential student's decision-making. PSDs will also allow new staff coming to work on a programme to find out about the course and how it has been planned so they are worth consulting before teaching on any programme. According to the QAA, a programme specification is *a concise description of the intended learning outcomes from an HE programme, and the means by which these outcomes are achieved and demonstrated*. Each individual HEI can decide what to include and in what order, but most PSDs include the following:

- name of the final award;
- programme title;
- details of accreditation by a professional body such as CIPD;
- UCAS code;
- aims of the programme;
- relevant QAA subject benchmark statements (see below);
- programme outcomes – usually written in terms of knowledge and understanding, skills, and other attributes;
- teaching, learning and assessment strategies involved on the programme;
- programme structures and requirements, levels, modules, credits and awards;
- date at which the programme specification was written or revised.

The PSD may also include other elements such as:

- admission criteria for potential students;
- learning and pastoral support available for students on the programme;
- methods for evaluating and improving the quality and standards of learning;

- work-based learning elements such as work placements;
- a description of distinctive features of the programme.

Although some of these elements are administrative, the PSD is essentially an academic document, which is usually written by the course leader or the course team. It should both describe and guide the planning of teaching and learning on the course. Writing and sub-sequently revising the document should allow the course team to reflect on the course and how it is taught and this should in turn help to identify areas that might be enhanced. The QAA does not stipulate a particular template for the PSD, though many institutions do have a set format to be followed for all of their courses in order to maintain consistency across their provision. If you need to create your own PSD, you should check with your awarding body or institution if there is a set structure or template to be followed before you start.

The PSD often forms the basis for the discussion during validation procedures although, as noted above, this was not the original purpose. Their evolution into institutional vali-dation documents may go some way to explain why PSDs can be rather complex and not readily comprehensible to the students for whom they were intended.

Subject benchmarks

In collaboration with the whole of the HE sector, the QAA has produced subject bench-mark statements for a wide range of subject disciplines which set out what achievement is expected according to the discipline and to the level of the programme. These benchmark statements are enormously helpful when you are creating a new course. According to the QAA, these benchmarks state, *what gives a discipline its coherence and identity, and define what can be expected of a graduate in terms of the abilities and skills needed to develop understanding or competence in the subject*. Some sets of statements combine or make reference to professional standards required by external professional or regulatory bodies in the discipline. The following come from the QAA statement for a degree in law.

Subject-specific abilities

Knowledge

6.1 A student should demonstrate a basic knowledge and understanding of the principal features of the legal system(s) studied. They should be able to:

- *demonstrate knowledge of a substantial range of major concepts, values, principles and rules of that system;*
- *explain the main legal institutions and procedures of that system;*
- *demonstrate the study in depth and in context of some substantive areas of the legal system.*

Application and problem solving

6.2 A student should demonstrate a basic ability to apply their knowledge to a situation of limited complexity in order to provide arguable conclusions for concrete problems (actual or hypothetical).

Some of the benchmarks are generic and aspects may be shared with a variety of quite diverse programmes. Again, the example below comes from the statement for law.

General transferable intellectual skills

Analysis, synthesis, critical judgement and evaluation

7.1 A student should demonstrate a basic ability to:

- *recognise and rank items and issues in terms of relevance and importance;*
- *bring together information and materials from a variety of different sources;*
- *produce a synthesis of relevant doctrinal and policy issues in relation to a topic;*
- *make a critical judgement of the merits of particular arguments;*
- *present and make a reasoned choice between alternative solutions.*

Autonomy and ability to learn

7.2 A student should demonstrate a basic ability, with limited guidance, to:

- *act independently in planning and undertaking tasks in areas of law which they have already studied;*
- *be able to undertake independent research in areas of law which they have not previously studied starting from standard legal information sources;*
- *reflect on their own learning, and to seek and make use of feedback.*

These benchmark statements are freely available on the QAA website (see Further Reading below) and you will be expected to refer to them during most validation processes. We will return briefly to the QAA benchmarks when we discuss quality assurance in the final chapter.

Writing programmes of study

Even if you are following a course provided by a different institution or awarding body it is very likely that you or your team will have to create some kind of course or programme document, even if just for the purposes of validation with the awarding body. For example, your college may be using Edexcel as the awarding body for HE qualifications. Edexcel do not provide a programme specification document. Instead they produce a range of optional units of study and the course team must select from these to form a coherent programme of study that meets the learning outcomes relating to the course's aims. This programme of study is then described in the programme specification document or equivalent.

The production of these documents requires knowledge of both national guidelines and, crucially, how these are locally interpreted. The awarding body or institution will very often produce extensive sets of regulations for courses, which are normally available through their website and which are regularly reviewed. You must ensure that you are fully aware of the most up-to-date regulations for the programme that you are developing.

Before writing the programme document it is worth being clear about whom you are writing for. Although the most obvious and pressing purpose may be some form of institutional validation or approval, as we have seen PSDs were initially expected to facilitate informed student choice. In any case, your students will have the right to read this document so its language and style should be accessible to them. There should be care of what prior understandings you assume, especially in the use of acronyms and other jargon. The QAA document, *Guidelines for Preparing Programme Specifications* suggests five questions around which to structure the course team's discussion on the development of programme specifications.

1. *What do we want out students to achieve?*

You may wish to refer to, for example, subject knowledge, skills, competency to practise and ethics. Eventually, what you want your learners to achieve will be written in the form of learning outcomes for the programme. The QAA suggests this process of identifying and refining the required learning will be helped by completing these sentences:

- This programme is distinctive because it develops...
- The most important values which inform this programme are...
- The academic content of this programme concentrates on...
- The most important intellectual skills developed in the programme are...
- The most useful practical skills, techniques and capabilities developed are...
- Competency will be developed in...
- The most important ways in which a student will learn are...
- On completing the programme we want students to know and understand...
- On completing the programme we want students to be able to...

2. *What reference points can we use to show that what we want students to achieve has currency within the academic, professional or employer communities?*

The answer to this question might come partly from your own institution's mission statements and policies. You should also consider:

- QAA subject benchmark statements;
- current research and scholarship in the field;
- requirements of relevant Professional, Statutory and Regulatory Bodies (PSBRs);
- relevant occupational standards;
- qualification descriptors used in the national qualifications framework.

3. *How should we use benchmark statements?*

The QAA is clear that these statements should not simply be transposed onto an institution's course document. *They are a point of comparison, a stimulus to reflection, and a reference against which individual programme specifications may be justified.* There is no compulsion to use them in specific ways. Nonetheless, since these benchmark statements were written by subject specialists they are invaluable for course teams who are forming their programme and its related documents.

4. *How do we expect our students to achieve and demonstrate the intended outcomes?*

The form of the assessment has a strong influence over the form of course delivery, so what type of learning do you want to promote? Essays are traditional in HE, but are they appropriate for every aspect of your course's assessment? How might the assessment strategy encourage active learning or the demonstration of appropriate professional skills? How might teamwork be incorporated in assessment, perhaps?

5. *Where can further information be found?*

PSDs are a concise summary of a course and what a student might expect while studying on that course, but these documents may also point to where further information or help about the organisation may be found. Many PSDs are available in electronic form (some are only available in electronic form and are held on the VLE) with links to course handbooks or information on computing and library services, for instance, so the student reading the document may be able to find more detailed information if required. QAA refers to these as 'layered' programme specifications.

The course team producing the programme specification document should also refer to *The UK Quality Code for Higher Education,* which is also produced by the QAA (see Chapter 9 and further reading). Remember, too, to be clear about the precise institutional stipulations for these documents and to make sure that you are using the most recent pro-forma.

Writing modules

As ever in HE, knowledge of local interpretation of national guidelines is important while writing new modules; your own institution may have its own pro-forma to be used, for example. Below is a typical module specification template, which will guide you on the kind of information that a module document requires. Remember, however, that the module specification should reflect the philosophy of the course and the module. In other words, the completion of the module document should only come after careful consideration of the learners, what they are going to learn and how they are going to learn it.

Table 4.1 Module specification institutional template

Module title	*Your institution may have guidelines on module titles to avoid duplication or overlap. Normally titles are brief and precise.*
Module code	*Your institution will normally give modules a code relating to level and discipline.*
Level	*At undergraduate level this may be foundation, intermediate or honours, for example.*
Credits or credit rating	*How many credits is this module worth? See above on credits and values.*
Study hours	*This is how much time you would expect a normal student to spend on this module. See above on notional study hours.*
Prerequisites (if any)	*Students may only take certain modules if they have passed other preliminary modules. For example, a student may have had to pass a research methods module before taking a dissertation module.*
Excluded combinations (if any)	*Students may not study some modules in combination, usually because there is significant overlap in their content.*
Recommended prior study	*Though not compulsory, which modules would you recommend students to have studied first?*
Module leader	*Who is in charge of managing the module?*

Rationale

This is a brief statement of the purpose and content of the module and may relate to the specific courses on which it is used.

Aims

These are broad statements which describe the main purpose of the module, which normally connects to the outcomes.

Learning outcomes

Statements of what a successful student will have demonstrated on completion of the module. These will very often include outcomes relating to knowledge and understanding, ability and key skills. Normally all module learning outcomes are assessed. See section below on writing outcomes.

Indicative content (or synopsis)

This is an outline of the content of the module. It may also include the approach to teaching and learning.

Key skills

This may describe the key skill involved in the completion of the module.

Assessment strategy

This will have information on the form of the assessment (e.g. essays, presentations, oral examinations). If the assessment is in more than one part, it may identify which outcomes are assessed by which part of the assessment. This section may also mention formative assessment opportunities.

Assessment criteria

These may be written in statements that relate directly to the module's learning outcomes. This section will explain the criteria against which the achievement of specific learning outcomes will be assessed.

Indicative reading

Often a more complete reading list will be provided to students so this will include some of the key texts to which the module will refer.

Writing learning outcomes in HE

As on any course, the learning outcomes in HE are statements of what the student will know or understand or be able to do on completion of some specified element of learning. They are a description of anticipated change on the part of the learner resulting from engaging with the module. The outcomes also relate to the assessment activities and criteria that permit a judgement to be made on how well the learner has achieved the anticipated change. This all appears quite neat and reasonable but there is a risk, especially at HE level, that outcomes can be reductive. That is, in attempting to define learning by something that is readily observable for the purposes of assessment, module writers may avoid critical thinking or conceptualisation. In other words, they may avoid some of what constitutes the very essence of higher-level learning. Again, this highlights the central importance of the philosophy of the course and how that informs the writing of modules. The careful selection of verbs for learning outcomes will, however, also go some way to addressing the risk of being reductive. The list that follows offers only a few suggestions for verbs to use in outcomes that pertain broadly to cognition. These illustrate how different aspects of learning, or anticipated changes, may be articulated.

- *Knowledge and understanding:* define, recognise, discuss, explain, order, select, describe.
- *Analysis:* analyse, categorise, distinguish, compare, critique, differentiate.
- *Synthesis and application:* elaborate, develop, apply, select, plan, construct.
- *Evaluation:* evaluate, compare, order, define, select.
- *Problem-solving:* recognise, rationalise, explain a decision, advocate, demonstrate.

More important, though, is to be precise in your thinking about what you want your students to learn and then try to articulate that as simply as possible without losing meaning or rigour.

Many module documents specify the expected word count for assignments. The number of words expected is a way of establishing the level of a module's demand and allows comparison to be made with other modules. For written assessments this is quite straightforward, it is simply the number of words that the essay or reflection or account must contain, often within a ten per cent range. Word count is more problematic when it is indicative, for instance in relation to presentations or practical tasks. Sometimes you might come across terms like 'word equivalence'. Institutions will often have their own guidelines but, broadly, word count will link to the credit value and to the number of study hours. The higher the credit level, the more study hours and the higher the word count.

Below are some further points to consider when writing module outcomes in HE.

- Consider the level of the module and what you would expect from a student working at that level. How much independent thinking or analysis would you expect, for instance?
- Use language the students can understand. If you use the word 'critical', be prepared to explain to your students what that entails (see Chapter 5) for the specific module.
- Limit the number of outcomes. If you are producing too many, that may suggest that the module is unwieldy and needs more focus.
- Examine your outcomes to judge whether they allow students to demonstrate critical analysis rather than just give a description of the topic. Do the outcomes demand appropriate academic challenge?

Module and programme approval

Having written your programme specification documents or your modules, you have to have them approved or validated by the awarding institution or body before they can be offered to students. For colleges or other educational organisations involved with a university in collaborative provision, there may be a requirement to be formally validated as an institutional partner. Typically, this involves making a lengthy written submission fulfilling certain criteria and agreeing to certain commitments. This written process is followed by a visit including a formal meeting with senior staff. The college or organisation will be required to map its own quality assurance processes to those stipulated by the university and to put in place new processes where there is nothing which corresponds. The regulations of the university or awarding body take precedence in relation to the course to be validated.

Having obtained approval as a collaborative partner where that is necessary, then the programme and module approval may proceed. Once again, this will usually involve a lengthy written submission, written in a given format, followed by a formal visit for a validation meeting or event. This event will often involve a brief presentation from the college and then representatives from the college will be asked questions on their submitted documentation. These questions may relate to the demand for the course (is it viable?), the resources available for learners or perhaps the qualifications or experience of the course team. After private deliberation the visitor from the awarding body or HEI will make a decision which may be given in terms of confidence or no confidence in the new course, or simply approval or non-approval. It is very common to receive approval subject to the fulfilment of certain stipulations. A variation of this process will take place as part of periodic reviews of the provision. Modules are usually approved as part of this general course validation, though new modules may go through a similar if less time-consuming process. Chapter 9 has more details of the quality assurance aspects of validation.

Working with prescribed programmes

You may find yourself teaching on courses where the content and the modules are written by the awarding body or HEI, which may also set out the precise pattern of delivery or even the resources used. The extent of prescription differs very significantly from one award provider to another. One effect of the National Student Survey has been that some HEIs have become especially concerned that all students who are studying towards the same qualification should have consistent access to resources, including teaching, regardless of where they take the course. This is considered as a matter of fairness: all students should have access to the same opportunities to learn whether based in the HEI or in a college. It may also, though, be driven by a concern that students will complain that they had not received what others had and so were disadvantaged. These sorts of concerns have become more acute now that students are being asked to pay very large sums for their courses, albeit not until they complete and even then only according to what they earn. In any case, it is important to ascertain what degree of autonomy you have in choices about teaching on prescribed courses. The nature and extent of scrutiny, support and independence depend upon the HEI or awarding body with which you are collaborating.

If you are working on a course that allows you the freedom to meet the course objectives as you consider appropriate, then you will make your own decisions about what resources and activities you use with the students. You may even be able to decide in what order you teach elements of the course. The qualification awarding institution may, though, have methods to share good practice or useful resources, often through a common VLE and these will be a good starter if you are just setting out. Within certain degree courses and some teacher education provision college providers meet regularly, every month or every term perhaps, to discuss courses and how they are taught. College providers may be asked to contribute their ideas about teaching activities or resources to these events, although these events can also become rather bureaucratic as new procedures are introduced and discussed. There may also be regular visits by staff from the awarding body or institution to liaise with course teams based in colleges. The quality of these courses where there is a high level of autonomy will ultimately be checked during events when students' work is moderated or externally verified.

At the other end of the spectrum of college-based HE, some courses will be run with much greater levels of prescription from the HEI or awarding body. The order of modules may be stipulated and even the resources and activities to be used with students. In some cases, staff from the HEI will carry out much or all of the teaching to ensure the consistency of the student experience as described earlier. This is still rare, however. Nevertheless, it is to be recommended that you and your colleagues clarify the expectations of the award provider and finding out the answer to these questions may help in this.

- Can we teach modules or course elements in any order?
- Can we choose the resources and activities to use with students?
- Can we decide how and/or when the students are assessed?
- How often will we receive visits from the awarder?
- How often will we need to attend at the awarder?

No matter what awarder you collaborate with, it is crucial that you are absolutely clear about when the assessment results are required so that your students can awarded with their credits and, finally, their qualification. Miss that date and your students may have to wait months before there is another opportunity.

A SUMMARY OF KEY POINTS

During this chapter, we have looked at the following key issues:
➤ How to make sense of modules and programmes, including the specific jargon they contain such as 'notional study hours' and 'credit level'. We considered what information the Programme Specification Documents (PSDs) include and their role in validation processes.
➤ How to use the QAA benchmark statements as well as other guidance available from the QAA. The QAA works in collaboration with HEIs to advise, rarely to stipulate or compel, and their material is invaluable.
➤ How to write modules and programmes of study, emphasising the importance of institutional rules and procedures that need to be followed. We also examined the range of autonomy that different providers allow the colleges with which they collaborate.

This can all seem very bureaucratic and preparing documents for validation or institutional approval is extremely time-consuming. So, when planning for teaching and learning it is worth returning to where this chapter began. We need to look beyond the documentation that every organisation demands to focus on what we want our students to learn and what values we want our courses to incorporate.

Branching options

Reflection

As you look back over this chapter, think about the courses that you teach on and how much autonomy you have. Can you make changes or alter the pattern of teaching, for example? Compare experiences of working on different college-based HE courses with colleagues. How do different providers organise their courses; how does the documentation differ? How do these different courses reflect the values on which they are based?

Analysis

How has the sequence of content been arranged on your courses? What do your students need to know or be able to do first? How does the planned programme enhance your students' motivation? Think about what Michael Young argued about knowledge. How does that idea of a body of knowledge relate to the HE courses you work on?

Research

Look at the QAA website and find the documents mentioned in this chapter. Read the *UK Quality Code for Higher Education* and examine how the concepts and standards there are reflected in the documentation for your course. How will your course need to evolve to keep meeting these criteria? Read the QAA benchmark statements for your subject to judge how your course meets these.

REFERENCES REFERENCES **REFERENCES** REFERENCES **REFERENCES**

Toohey, S. (1999) *Designing Courses for Higher Education.* London: Society for Research into Higher Education.
Young, M. (2008) *Bringing Knowledge Back in: From Social Constructivism to Social Realism in the Sociology of Education.* London: Taylor & Francis.
The QAA website (www.qaa.ac.uk) has links to many of the documents discussed in this chapter including the subject benchmark statements, *The UK Quality Code for Higher Education* and *Guidelines for Preparing Programme Specifications*.

5

The practice of teaching college-based higher education

By the end of this chapter you will be able to:

- critically evaluate research into HE taught in FE contexts;
- critically evaluate some key concepts in teaching and learning in HE courses;
- apply key concepts to a range of teaching situations on HE courses.

Introduction

What is good teaching in HE? There can be no single answer to that important question because what is 'good' will depend on a variety of factors specific to the circumstances of the teaching such as the students, the course or the institutional environment. What constitutes good teaching is certainly complex, but that does not mean it is mysterious. As with other areas of scholarship it should be possible to analyse and discuss teaching without reducing it to the simplistic and general. At the very least it seems reasonable that HE teachers in colleges, like those elsewhere, should be able to articulate what they are doing to facilitate student learning and why they are doing it. Perhaps, even that bland statement needs some examination, however. Gert Biesta (2009, page 3) has lamented the conflation of learning and education, which he refers to as *learnification*. For Biesta, education implies a relationship between teachers and students that emphasises content whereas learning is a process that emphasises merely the individual. What Biesta calls 'learnification' reflects the circumstances of many courses today where gaining credentials, such as a degree certificate, appears more important than what has been learned. We will return to this when we examine deep and surface learning below. Nevertheless, the relationship between knowledge content and a student's broader intellectual development is a significant concern for the HE teacher.

This chapter will discuss the teacher's role and so will deliberately lay the stress on teaching. Let us start, though, by posing the question, *what do we mean by learning?* Despite the current rhetorical stress on learning and the learner, to which Biesta alludes, it is surprising how rarely this fundamental concept is discussed. Policymakers, textbooks and curriculum documents all refer to learning as if it were unproblematic and as if there were unquestioned agreement of what it entails. Some clarity about what we mean by learning will help us to understand our role as HE teachers and what we are planning for our students to do or comprehend. Knud Illeris's (2007, page 3) definition is a good place to start. He defined learning as *any process that in living organisms leads to permanent capacity change and which is not solely due to biological maturation or ageing*. This is very broad, maybe too broad to help educators understand their role.

Moreover, it is certainly arguable that people can forget what they have learnt because change through learning may not be permanent. How many of us remember everything we learned at school? Nonetheless, the focus on change in capacity remains useful, which does not necessarily imply competence in a practical hands-on sense, though it may do. Change in capacity may also refer to cognition or even empathy, but it indicates that the learner engages with what they are learning. Frank Coffield's (2008, page 7) definition of learning is similar to that of Illeris but more precise and probably more helpful for an educator.

Learning refers only to significant changes in capability, understanding, knowledge, practices, attitudes or values by individuals, groups, organisations or society. Two qualifications. It excludes the acquisition of factual information when it does not contribute to such changes; it also excludes immoral learning as when prisoners learn from other inmates in custody how to extend their repertoire of criminal activities.

Teachers are looking for significant changes and not just within the individual. Though this definition excludes immoral learning, it is worth remembering that our students can learn what we might not plan for them to and that people can learn things that are wrong. More productively, Coffield's list of changes (*capability, understanding, knowledge, practices, attitudes or values*) can get us to be precise about the change in our students that we are seeking to effect through our HE sessions. We then need to consider what level that change needs to be at for students on HE courses.

CLOSE FOCUS **CLOSE** FOCUS **CLOSE** FOCUS **CLOSE** FOCUS **CLOSE** FOCUS

What do we mean by 'being critical'?

Students are constantly told to be critical in HE, sometimes without adequate explanation of what being critical means. Of course, criticality is a slippery concept but if we are to demand it from our students we need at least to be able to express what it involves. We are not helped, however, by the everyday meaning of being critical, which is to find fault. Criticality may indeed involve finding fault, but that is not the intention of critical thinking.

When we ask students to be critical we are asking them to make an informed analysis of a given topic, which will explain why something is as it is. The analysis will normally be informed by scholarship, which fundamentally means reading and understanding the work of other writers on the topic; what academics often refer to as 'the literature'. The analysis will also normally have a logical structure that ensures it examines the topic thoroughly.

None of this is easy, but the section below on deep and surface approaches may help in planning teaching to encourage students to think critically.

No matter what the subject we would especially expect HE students to develop their intellectual capacity. That is, we would expect them to think critically, to look beneath the simplicity of the surface to the complexity of what is below, no matter what subject we are teaching. To encourage that criticality, this chapter will discuss some theories and approaches that have explained and informed teaching practice in HE.

Thinking about your own practice, what do you understand by learning? What changes do you plan for your students to experience as a result of your sessions?

Does your practice differ between HE and FE level students?

Current research into HE in FE: summaries and implications for practice

A study by June and David Harwood (2004) found that a majority of college-based HE teachers they surveyed who taught at both FE and HE levels stated that their practice was different on HE courses. Their respondents were, however, vague when describing just how their practice was different. This finding reflects a wider confusion on what, if anything, makes teaching HE in an FE context distinctive. Some argue that the college context allows teachers to use a wider variety of approaches than their colleagues in universities. Classes in colleges are often smaller and teaching spaces more flexible than a university's lecture theatres, for example. Perceptions of teaching may be deceptive. A quantitative analysis of HE practice in a network of 17 FE colleges in the southwest of England carried out by Sue Burkill, Sue Rodway-Dyer and Mark Stone found evidence of students being taught in lectures based around the transmission of knowledge in a fairly traditional manner. Yet, at the same time, the teachers running these lectures described their approach as student-centred and flexible. These researchers argued that *HE in FE teachers operate in a context which, despite some external constraints, gives them considerable flexibility in the choice of teaching approaches* (2008, page 329). It could be, though, that the use of traditional lecturing is an effort to give students a more 'genuine' HE experience. That is to say, teachers in FE may be conforming to what is perceived as 'normal' in HE, which is popularly characterised by a formal didactic lecture. In any case, to develop our teaching we need to examine our assumptions and our perceptions. This chapter is written with that intention.

What does criticality look like in your subject area? How does it differ from description? Thinking about a particular element of your subject, what specific questions might you ask to encourage students' critical thinking?

Working with adult and non-traditional undergraduates

As we shall see in the final chapter, college-based HE has been specifically praised for welcoming students who might not otherwise have attended university-level courses, never mind university. HE in FE students are as diverse as the settings in which they are taught. Students on a full-time foundation degree may have come straight from school while students on a part-time professional development degree may be returning to education after decades away from formal classes. HE in FE students are, however, almost certain to be adults. Some educators talk about teaching adults as if they are a homogenous group and as if teaching adults is a practice quite distinct from teaching children. For example, some initial teacher education courses for FE focus on the work of Malcolm Knowles (1980) and his concept of adult teaching and learning known as 'andragogy'. Knowles argues that at a certain point of maturation virtually all humans become self-directing or autonomous. Andragogy, as opposed to pedagogy, involves developing this self-direction by adapting programmes to the articulated needs of learners. This, so Knowles's argument goes, enhances adults' motivation. Directing the adult on what to do, by contrast, is de-motivating and establishes a block to adults' learning. Adult learners are, according to this understanding, essentially self-motivated and well able to convey their needs to their educator, whose role it is to fulfil those needs. Allied to this is the assumption that adult learning is always liberational and inherently enjoyable. Stephen Brookfield (1996) dismisses these ideas as myths and argues convincingly that it is context and biography rather than lifespan that matter most in how we learn. As Alan Rogers and Naomi Horrocks (2010, page 81) put it, *new students are not new people*. Our learners will have developed knowledge, values and attitudes through their experiences. As a result, adults are likely to have certain expectations of how they will be treated and taught and this is especially the case with students on higher-level courses. Some adult learners will want to be closely directed, especially if they are returning to education. Rather than there being a single point of 'becoming' an autonomous learner, adults continue to develop and learn. No learner, however, wishes to be patronised.

Accepting, then, that our students are not a homogenous group, we can make some tentative observations about those students who are returning to education after a significant time. In this context it is useful to note how society's expectations of education have evolved and how this evolution might motivate older people to return to education. The 'massification' of HE is a recent phenomenon in the UK and consequently many older people will have joined professions that are now degree entry, such as nursing, with lower qualifications. As more young people move into the workplace with HE qualifications, some older people will have found that there are now barriers to promotion without a degree. For these and similar reasons people may seek out college-based HE courses which are often more convenient and flexible in order to progress their career. FE is rightly celebrated as the home of the second chance in education, especially at HE level. This return to education may be instantly inspiring for some older students, but for others it can mean re-visiting past failure. Finding the balance between making these students feel confident that they can succeed while still providing rigorous challenge may be difficult, but it is key to successful HE teaching. This is not to argue for a form of therapeutic education for non-traditional students that simply makes them feel good regardless of their intellectual development, as criticised by Ecclestone and Hayes (2008). Rather, this is to suggest that teaching be sequenced to ensure that what is being asked of students is neither too easy nor beyond their comprehension at any point in the course.

We should be aware, too, that education has its own technical requirements and jargon, especially around assessment, which can divert those returning to education away from what is most important in their academic development. A good example of this might be citation and referencing in written assignments. Passing off someone else's work as your own, plagiarism, is a very serious offence in HE and so it is crucial that students learn to cite references accurately and consistently. Yet, when there has been no attempt to plagiarise, we should avoid providing feedback that emphasises the technicalities of referencing above all else. Such feedback is easy for teachers to give because it is technical and specific, but, however necessary it may be, such feedback is not about what is fundamental to HE.

Theories of learning and teaching in HE

Implicit in this chapter and in this book is the idea that we should enquire about the impact of our teaching on our students. The work of John Hattie (2009) among others has pointed to the huge effect that the teacher has on the learning of students: he has found strong evidence that the approach and skills of the teacher are central to students succeeding. That is still the case with students on higher-level courses where the student is expected to have greater autonomy. However, it is important to stress that the individual teacher is not the only determinant of a student's success, nor even the most important one. The student's educational experience and social background, their support, their aspirations and their motivation all have very significant effects on achievement, though teachers have little or no control over many of these factors. That needs to be stressed because otherwise teachers in HE, as elsewhere, can feel guilty or be blamed for what they cannot influence. Moreover, an apathetic member of the teaching team can scupper the efforts of more enthusiastic colleagues. Nevertheless, what we do in the classroom or workshop as teachers is crucial, and while we may not be able to influence our students' social background we can inform and develop our own practice. In that spirit this section examines some theories that are relevant to pedagogy in HE. We can understand educational theory to be a coherent set of ideas that explains or defines particular phenomena. Here we are going to examine just three theories related to education: deep and surface learning, zones of proximal development and communities of practice. These are well-established concepts in education, though they continue to be developed and they have proved to be useful for teachers in HE settings. Many others could have been chosen and you may well want to research your own ways to think about teaching and learning. To be clear from the outset, though, the point of educational theory is to challenge and extend our practice, not just to lend a name to what we already do.

RESEARCH FOCUS   RESEARCH FOCUS   RESEARCH FOCUS   RESEARCH FOCUS

Deep and surface learning

Ference Marton and Roger Säljö first introduced the influential concept of deep and surface learning in an article published in 1976, which described students' approaches to learning in particular situations. These concepts remain a very useful way to categorise and so to think about how students learn and, perhaps more significantly, to identify what we as their teachers expect from our students. Marton and Säljö set out to examine how HE students approached everyday activities on their courses. They asked a group of students to read an academic article and told them they would have to answer questions on it. They found that some students approached the text as a collection of discrete units of information to be memorised in order to answer the anticipated questions. They called this the 'surface approach' to learning. Other students treated the text as having coherence and a meaning relevant to them. Marton and Säljö called this the 'deep approach' to learning.

Deep and surface learning

A broad description of the characteristics of deep and surface approaches to learning is set out below.

Deep learning:

- The intention is to understand key concepts or meanings.
- Relates knowledge derived from different parts of the course or from different sources into a coherent whole.
- New knowledge is related to established knowledge.
- Identification of patterns and principles to inform conclusions.
- Abstract or theoretical knowledge is related to everyday experience.
- The task is seen as a means to develop knowledge.

Surface learning:

- The intention is to complete the task.
- Parts of the task are not related in a logical manner and coherence is not sought.
- Failure to identify patterns or principles.
- Information is memorised, especially for the purpose of assessment.
- The task is seen as an imposition in itself.

It is important to stress that these descriptors relate to the student's approach to learning, not to the student themselves nor even to their capacity to learn. As Paul Ramsden (2003, page 62) who has developed Marton and Säljö's ideas has argued: *Deep and surface approaches are responses to the educational environments in which students learn.* Students generally do what they think will bring them reward or achievement. So, the form of assessment we adopt is crucial; if we set tasks that demand surface learning, that is what we can expect. The words of American mathematician and educator W. W. Sawyer (1943, page 8) help to illustrate this distinction between surface and deep or what he refers to here as the subject and its imitation:

> *Nearly every subject has a shadow, or imitation. It would, I suppose, be quite possible to teach a deaf and dumb child to play the piano. When it played a wrong note, it would see the frown of its teacher, and try again. But it would obviously have no idea of what it was doing, or why anyone should devote hours to such an extraordinary exercise. It would have learnt an imitation of music. And it would fear the piano exactly as most students fear what is supposed to be mathematics.*

> *What is true of music is also true of other subjects. One can learn imitation history — kings and dates, but not the slightest idea of the motives behind it all; imitation literature — stacks of notes on Shakespeare's phrases, and a complete destruction of the power to enjoy Shakespeare.*

Deep learning is about the coherent whole and deep learning has personal meaning and relevance. Marton and Säljö did not, however, place a judgement of value on either deep or surface learning because they considered these approaches to learning as rational responses to specific situations. If a student has not revised for an exam then surface learning through cramming the night before is appropriate. Similarly, rote learning can be entirely appropriate. A statistician has to remember sets of formulae and analytical techniques, which may be efficiently retained through rote learning. Those formulae and techniques do not, though, define how a statistician thinks. Nevertheless, we can reasonably say that we are more likely to want deep approaches to learning from our HE students and we cannot teach deep learning skills if shallow skills are rewarded. Deep learning is, furthermore, more likely to engage our students' interest and ultimately be more fulfilling. Ramsden (2003, page 80) set out approaches to teaching in HE that are associated with deep and surface learning as below.

Surface approaches are encouraged by:

- assessment that emphasises recall or the application of trivial procedural knowledge;
- assessment methods that create anxiety;
- cynical or conflicting messages about rewards;
- an excessive amount of material in the curriculum;
- poor or no feedback on progress;
- lack of independence in studying;
- lack of interest or background in the subject taught;
- previous educational experience that has encouraged surface approaches.

Deep approaches are encouraged by:

- teaching and assessment methods that foster active and long-term engagement with learning activities;
- stimulating and considerate teaching that demonstrates the teacher's commitment to the subject matter and which stresses meaning and relevance to students;
- clearly stated academic expectations;
- opportunities to exercise responsible choice in the method and content of study;
- interest in and background knowledge of the subject matter;
- previous experiences of education that has encouraged deep approaches to learning.

Clearly, the teacher cannot affect all of these but good teaching at HE level encourages deep approaches to learning, which can engage students critically with the subject and which can unlock their understanding. This means thinking about how students can be encouraged to critically engage with the content and so it means being clear about what we want students to learn. It also demands the teacher's enthusiasm.

This theorisation of surface and deep approaches to learning articulates well with the next concept we consider, zones of proximal development.

Social constructivism and zones of proximal development

The ideas of the social constructivist Lev Vygotsky have made the unlikely journey from obscurity in Stalinist Russia in the 1920s and 1930s to mainstream orthodoxy throughout Western education today (see the research focus below). The concept of the Zone of Proximal Development (ZPD) is perhaps Vygotsky's most commonly used one although he actually wrote little about it. Nonetheless, its elegant simplicity and explanatory power have sustained, even though the ZPD concept has expanded well beyond its origins in Vygotsky's study of assessment and instruction in childhood development. The ZPD can basically be defined as the space between what a learner can do on their own and what they cannot do even with expert help. It is the dynamic and shifting space within which learning takes place. As learning occurs, so the learner's ZPD shifts up because the learner can do more on their own (see Figure 5.1). A toddler learning to walk initially needs to hold an adult's hands. This supported practice allows the toddler to gain the individual ability to walk independently. Similarly, learners need support but, like the toddler learning to walk, learners also need that support to be withdrawn in order to gain independence.

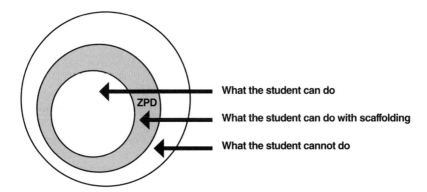

Figure 5.1   The Zone of Proximal Development

The emphasis within the ZPD is not, however, on the transfer of skills from the more capable or knowledgeable partner (in our case, the teacher) to the learner. Rather, it is on the creation and development of meaning for the learner through collaboration with the expert. Though it is a term never used by Vygotsky himself, this temporary support provided by the expert or teacher within the ZPD has been referred to as *scaffolding*. This idea is central to teaching, especially teaching difficult content as on HE courses. These related concepts of the ZPD and scaffolding help to identify how the role of the HE teacher is contingent upon the learner's individual situation and needs. In terms that are particularly relevant to the teacher in an HE setting, Jerome Bruner (1997, page 69; quoted in Daniels, 2001, pages 207–8) suggests how the teacher might form the scaffolding through *shielding a learner from distraction, by fore fronting crucial features of a problem, by sequencing the steps to understanding, by promoting negotiation.* Others have described how the role of the teacher in the ZPD is to support the learner by reducing the uncertainty around a task contingent upon the responses of the individual learner. David Wood suggests five levels of levels of prompts to support learners in this way (1986, pages 197–8):

- Level 0: no assistance.
- Level 1: general verbal prompt ('What might you do here?').
- Level 2: specific verbal prompt ('You might use your computer tools here').
- Level 3: indicates materials ('Why not use a graph plotter?').
- Level 4: prepares materials (tutor selects and sets up tools).
- Level 5: demonstrates use of tools.

So, contingent upon the learner's correct responses or actions the teacher reduces the level of control. If the learner makes a mistake, the tutor raises the level of control. Thus, the scaffolding will be raised or removed. As Wood's examples indicate, the precise form of the scaffolding, and hence the form of the teacher's prompts, depends upon the subject matter and the task in hand. That means the teacher's role as knowledge-able expert is crucial, not just their capacity to facilitate. The teacher must comprehend the body of knowledge, so as to sequence and highlight what is most salient to help students to learn. Moreover, Vygotsky makes the distinction between what he calls scientific knowledge and spontaneous or 'everyday' knowledge. In other words, the understanding that a group of novices will develop alone does not have the value of expert knowledge that has been systematically researched and acquired. Teaching based on the concept of the ZPD is not about making students feel more confident about their limited knowledge; it is about allowing students access to 'scientific' knowledge in such a way that they can internalise, adapt and apply it themselves.

REFLECTIVE TASK

Think about an element of your subject that is particularly demanding. How might you sequence its introduction to students within a ZPD? Which components would students initially need to grasp to allow them to progress towards independent knowledge? What responses or actions would indicate to you that a student has understood the fundamentals of this element? What prompts might you give a student as part of the scaffolding?

Theorising HE teaching in this way can link to promoting deep learning as discussed in the previous section. It can guide the planning of a student's progress by focusing on what we want them to learn, depending upon their level, by reducing uncertainty and through initially shielding them from distraction. This seems particularly important for adult and non-traditional students returning to education who need to be challenged but not thwarted. The concept of the ZPD locates where that challenge should occur for each student.

RESEARCH FOCUS

Lev Semyonovitch Vygotsky's ideas have considerable authority in the study and practice of education across the world. His understanding that learning is fundamentally a social activity mediated by cultural 'tools', most importantly language, is behind concepts such as Lave and Wenger's communities of practice and Engeström's expansive learning. Vygotsky's background was, though, inauspicious. He was born in Belorussia in 1896 to a middle-class and well-educated Jewish family. As a teenager his intellectual interests lay in literature but at his parent's insistence he attended the Medical School of Moscow University. In his first semester there he transferred to studying law, though his PhD, completed in 1925, was on the psychology of art. During the time that Vygotsky was studying in Moscow all that was solid was melting into air with the circulation of new ideas in the arts, sciences and politics culminating in the October revolution of 1917. This transformation of society at first allowed Vygotsky to become influential both in the development of psychological theory and its application. In the early 1930s, however, with Stalin firmly in power and tightening his grip over every aspect of society, Vygotsky and his ideas lost favour as they were considered individualistic and bourgeois. He died of tuberculosis in 1934 and his writings only became widely available outside Russia in the 1970s. Among the numerous works that explain and apply Vygotsky's work, Harry Daniels (2001) provides an excellent overview of Vygotsky's contribution to pedagogy.

Communities of practice

The concept of communities of practice first developed by Jean Lave and Etienne Wenger in 1991 is an attempt to theorise how people learn from experience in the workplace. Experiential learning does not involve teaching in a traditional sense so it may seem odd that we are discussing it here. Many students on college-based HE courses, however, take professional development courses while they are working, such as is the case with in-service teacher training or high-level accountancy courses. These students combine academic study with their experiential knowledge gained in the workplace and it may be difficult to distinguish what they learn in which setting. It is sensible, therefore, for the HE teacher to at least be aware of theories around work-based learning, such as communities of practice, and we will turn later to how the HE teacher might use this theorisation to inform their teaching.

The term communities of practice, coined by Lave and Wenger in 1991, focuses on learning beyond formal training and qualifications to how knowledge, skills and capacities are developed in the workplace through the relationships people have there. Groups of people who are occupied in similar and related activities in the workplace may constitute a community of practice and people develop new skills and knowledge through involvement with that community. Lave and Wenger borrowed three understandings from Vygotsky for their theory:

- What we learn relates to what we already know as well as to what we do not know.
- Knowledge is formed and held in social relations; that is, by groups of people.
- Learning is situated in a particular space and time.

Together, these understandings suggest that groups of people in the workplace do not just provide a venue for learning. Rather, groups of people in the workplace are the means whereby learning happens. Lave and Wenger describe this process of learning as legitimate peripheral participation, whereby established workers allow some marginal engagement to newcomers in the workplace. As the newcomers' participation in the community grows, so their skill, knowledge and enculturation develop. Learning inevitably occurs as a consequence of participation within a community of practice but those who are the most skilful learners have a *prereflective grasp of complex situations* and *the ability to improvise* (Lave and Wenger, 1991, page 20). Not every group of people working together constitutes a community of practice, however. Wenger's later development of the concept isolates three identifying elements: mutual engagement; joint enterprise; and shared repertoire (Wenger, 1998, pages 73–85). Communities develop over time and they require mutual engagement from the members. Lave and Wenger also describe how learning involves becoming a different person, it *involves the construction of identities* (Lave and Wenger, 1991, page 53). This is especially apparent on professional courses as students make the transition to identifying themselves with the profession they are to join.

How might HE tutors based in a college use this concept in their own practice? Some teachers like to think of their own groups of students as communities of practice to encourage mutual development, but this may stretch the concept beyond its useful boundaries. Nonetheless, the concept does help us comprehend how people learn from each other, for better or for worse. Communities of practice are not necessarily benign and they may promote knowledge that is outmoded or reactionary, for example. We can perhaps find more purposeful application of the concept in comprehending and enhancing the relationship between academic course and professional practice.

As mentioned above, college-based HE students often study part-time while they work within the role they are developing. They therefore have the opportunity to integrate what they learn from formal study with what they learn through more informal practical experience. Knowledge of theories of experiential learning can help to inform planning for professional courses so that taught classes complement the students' work-based learning. The concept of communities of practice gives us a vocabulary to discuss the workplace, beginning with asking the students whether they think such a community exists where they work. We may not be able to teach students to develop a *prereflective grasp of complex situations* and *the ability to improvise* that Lave and Wenger described were characteristics of the skilful learner; we may, though, be able to simulate situations that the student will encounter in the workplace to analyse what determines decision-making there. We can, furthermore, take situations from the students' own experience of the workplace and examine them in class to learn about what happened.

Reflective practice is commonly an integral element of college-based HE and structured reflective writing is commonly an element of students' final assessment. Thinking about experiential learning theory, such as communities of practice, may help students to recognise and reflect on their own development in the workplace while they have been on the course. How has their identity changed? How do they relate differently to colleagues? What do they take for granted in the work setting that seemed strange at first? What technical or workplace-specific vocabulary have they assimilated into their own vocabulary? In other words, successfully applying concepts like communities of practice brings the workplace into the college course.

REFLECTIVE TASK

What communities of practice do you belong to? What are their identifying features – their boundaries, their signs of membership or their ways of talking? What have you learnt from participating in these communities?

Principles of good teaching

Below are some principles of good teaching that are adapted from Kember and McKight (2007). These may help to guide your approach to teaching in HE, but they are only meant as a stimulus for your own principles.

1. Teaching should address the future needs of students. What do your students need to understand and be able to do? This implies more than content and extends to their general capabilities including:

    - capacity to learn independently;
    - critical thinking;
    - analytical skills;
    - collaboration;
    - leadership;
    - communication.

2. Teaching should allow students access to a thorough understanding of the subject's fundamental concepts. That may mean covering less content.

3. Teaching should be made relevant. Getting students to engage with what they are learning enhances their motivation. This might involve:

   - using examples from real life. Vocational courses in particular need to maintain a clear line of sight to the workplace;
   - demonstrating how theory and practice interact symbiotically.

4. Teaching should actively involve students. Consider what activities will engage students in their learning.

5. Teaching should challenge assumptions. Students should be encouraged to articulate and justify what they believe.

6. Teachers should treat their students as individuals, not as parts of a homogenous group. Learn and use your students' names as a first step to getting to know them.

7. Good teaching can enhance motivation.

   - Choose relevant materials to use with groups.
   - Your own enthusiasm can be powerful.
   - Vary your approaches with groups.

8. Good teaching means giving effective feedback. Be specific about how students can improve their work in formative feedback.

9. Assess what is important, not just what is simple to assess.

A SUMMARY OF KEY POINTS

During this chapter we have looked at the following key issues:
- ➤ Theoretical frameworks for analysing teaching and learning in HE.
- ➤ The implications of these frameworks for practical approaches to teaching and learning.

Teaching in HE, as in any other sector, should usually derive from the response to two questions. The first is: what do I want my students to learn? And the second is: how best will they learn it? The answer to the first question will come from the course curriculum or syllabus and, above all, your own subject expertise. The answer to the second will depend on your students, your values and your knowledge of pedagogy. Arguably, this knowledge will never be complete, but it should always form a part of the practitioner's ongoing professional learning and reflection.

Branching options

Reflection

As you look back over this chapter, think about what you want your students to learn. Discuss this with colleagues at your college to see if you agree and also talk to colleagues at the awarding body or at the awarding university. How will your students be different if they do learn as you plan? Is meeting the course criteria the most important thing or is there more to what you want your students to know and experience? Reflect on your own specialist knowledge and consider which areas of knowledge you would prioritise for delivery to your students.

Analysis

The theories we have looked at offer only a glimpse at the huge range of ideas and concepts around learning and teaching. As professional teachers, we all should reflect on what we mean by learning and how that relates to our teaching practice. This can and should be informed by reading and weighing up what educational researchers have found, not just based on the unexamined notion of 'what works for me'. What are your understandings of learning? What are these founded upon? Is there a moral or ethical element to teaching and learning? Do you teach differently to how you were taught?

Research

Educational theory almost always derives from research, but that research is not of uniform good quality. Look at how theories like communities of practice or andragogy have developed; look at what writers base their theories on. Do they have sufficient evidence to make a convincing case? What criteria do you use to critique ideas around teaching and learning?

REFERENCES   REFERENCES   REFERENCES   REFERENCES

Biesta, G. (2009) Good Education: What It is and Why We Need It. Inaugural lecture. Stirling Institute of Education: 4 March. (available at http://www.ioe.stir.ac.uk/documents/GOODEDUCATION--WHATITISANDWHYWENEEDITInauguralLectureProfGertBiesta.pdf)

Brookfield, S. (1996) Adult Learning: An Overview, in A. Tuinjman (ed.) *International Encyclopedia of Education.* Oxford, Pergamon Press.

Burkill, S., Rodway-Dyer, S.J. and Stone, M. (2008) Lecturing in higher education in further education settings, *Journal of Further and Higher Education*, 32 (4): 321–31.

Coffield, F. (2008) *Just Suppose Teaching and Learning Became the First Priority...* London: LSN.

Daniels, H. (2001) *Vygotsky and Pedagogy.* London: RoutledgeFalmer.

Ecclestone, K. and Hayes, D. (2008) *The Dangerous Rise of Therapeutic Education*. London: Routledge.

Harwood, J. and Harwood, D. (2004) Higher education in further education: delivering higher education in a further education context – a study of five South West colleges, *Journal of Further and Higher Education,* 28 (2): 153–64.

Hattie, J. (2009) *Visible Learning: A Synthesis of Over 800 Meta-Analyses Relating to Achievement*. Abingdon: Routledge.

Illeris, K. (2007) *How We Learn?* Abingdon: Routledge.

Kember, D. and McKight, C. (2007) *Enhancing University Teaching: Lessons from Research into Award-Winning Teachers.* London: Routledge.

Knowles, M.S. (1980) *The Modern Practice of Adult Education: From Pedagogy to Andragogy,* Englewood Cliffs: Prentice Hall/Cambridge.

Lave, J. and Wenger, E. (1991) *Situated Learning: Legitimate Peripheral Participation*. Cambridge: Cambridge University Press.

Marton, F. and Säljö, R. (1997) Approaches to Learning, in F. Marton, D. Hounsell and N. Entwistle (eds) *The Experience of Learning. Implications for Teaching and Studying in Higher Education*. Edinburgh: Scottish Academic Press.

Ramsden, P. (2003) *Learning to Teach in Higher Education.* London: RoutledgeFalmer.

Rogers, A. and Horrocks, N. (2010) *Teaching Adults* (4th edition). Maidenhead: McGrawHill/Open University Press.

Sawyer, W.W. (1943) *Mathematician's Delight*. Harmondsworth: Penguin.

Vygotsky, L.S. (1978) *Mind in Society: The Development of Higher Psychological Processes.* Cambridge, MA: Harvard University Press.

Wood, D.J. (1986). Aspects of Teaching and Learning, in M. Richards and P. Light (eds) *Children of Social Worlds: Development in a Social Context.* Cambridge, MA: Harvard University Press.

6

Assessing learning in HE in FE

By the end of this chapter you will be able to:

- define relevant key concepts and terms relating to assessment and feedback in HE, and relate these to college-based provision;
- critically evaluate current debates and controversies relating to assessment practice in HE;
- identify current debates and controversies within college-based contexts.

Introduction

The assessment of students' learning is as central an aspect of HE as it is of FE. Both sectors face similar public, institutional and academic pressures. Employers need to have confidence in HE courses that prepare students for the world of work. Colleges and universities draw on the results of formal, summative assessment as indicators of the wider quality of teaching and students' learning. And teaching staff need to be confident that the assessment tasks which they design and grade are robust, reliable and valid. Clearly, the overarching concerns that shape conversations about assessment practice in FE are largely shared in HE. The fundamental theoretical foundations of assessment practice are similarly shared across these two sectors. Definitions of validity, reliability, authenticity and sufficiency of assessment are in essence identical whether referring to a portfolio at level 3 or an essay at level 5. Key principles of constructive, timely and meaningful feedback are also common across these sectors.

For the HE in FE lecturer, assessment practice in and of itself should not at first look present any complex theoretical or practical issues. Assessment validity is assessment validity, irrespective of the educational sector under discussion. Timely, constructive and clearly written feedback is of obvious importance to both the student at level 2 and the student completing a foundation degree. And while some of the terminology might be different – in HE we have external examiners rather than external verifiers and second marking instead of internal moderation, for example – the processes involved are simple to compare. So it should be straightforward for the FE lecturer to move to teaching and assessing within a HE in FE programme, shouldn't it?

Well, yes and no. It seems right to say that if a lecturer is capable of giving timely and clearly understandable feedback to a student at level 3, she can do the same for a student at level 4. And if a lecturer can interpret and then provide guidance for students relating to the assessment requirements for a first diploma, then carrying out a similar process for a foundation degree should also be a straightforward task. So (and this is a point of view that the authors have heard expressed by many college managers during recent years) assessment in HE in FE is not any harder or more troublesome than assessment in mainstream FE, right?

Well, not quite. There are in fact a number of current themes or debates in HE assessment practice, which raise difficult questions for lecturers in the HE sector and, therefore, for lecturers in the HE in FE sector as well. Above and beyond the fact that teaching HE requires the lecturer to have a critical, up-to-date and profound knowledge of the subject area being taught, there are other troublesome aspects of assessment practice that have an impact on how assessment gets done. The changing relationship between lecturer and student is one: the requirement of HE to produce more independent learners requires careful instruction and can cause difficulties. The nature of assessment decision making is another: should lecturers mark to learning outcomes, to assessment tasks, or make holistic judgements as to the quality of a piece of written work? Debates and practices such as these are complex and controversial and need to be recognised by HE in FE lecturers.

This chapter is divided into two main parts, therefore. To begin, we will briefly go over those key elements of assessment theory that underpin all good assessment practice from FE through to HE. After this, our attention will turn to a select number of current debates in HE assessment theory and practice which will be briefly explored in order to highlight the continuing debates that characterise HE assessment and which, we argue, ought also to be considered by HE in FE lecturers as well.

Assessment: principles, theory and practice

There are many books and journal articles that define and explore key terms and concepts in assessment practice in detail, providing worked examples and guidelines to good practice. References to some of these works appear at the end of this chapter. Here, we shall provide a relatively brief outline of these concepts. For the purposes of this discussion, we propose that the definitions and ideas put forward here apply equally to the HE sector as to the FE sector.

Initial and diagnostic assessment

There is some overlap between these two modes of assessment. Initial assessment is assessment that takes place either before or at the start of a programme of study. It is used to provide initial guidance and advice and to identify that the (prospective) student meets any required entry criteria for the programme of study in question. It may also be used to explore any possible claims for exemption of parts of the programme to be followed through the accreditation of prior learning/experience. Such initial assessment has a clear diagnostic function, therefore.

Diagnostic assessment can take place before or during a programme of study. It is used to review student progress (perhaps through tutorials and the use of an individual learning plan or portfolio of assessment), to highlight any strengths or development needs, or to assess and plan for any specific learning difficulties or disabilities that the student may have. Sometimes these will have been assessed during a prior programme of study, but for many students such issues may only emerge once they begin their studies in the further or HE sectors.

Formative and summative assessment

Formative assessment is often referred to as assessment *for* learning. It is assessment that takes place during a programme of study as an integral part of the learning process.

That is to say, rather than primarily aiming to generate grades or formal records of certification, formative assessment is designed to encourage learning, to provide opportunities for reinforcement or revision, and to provide feedback (discussed below) to both student and teacher about how the course is going. Formative assessment can be formal (students might be asked to write an essay or give a presentation to their peers), or informal (through the use of techniques such as question-and-answer or brainstorming).

Summative assessment is often referred to as assessment *of* learning. It is assessment that takes place at different points in the programme of study. Summative assessment is used to see if students have acquired the theoretical knowledge, body of skills or changes in attitude and aptitude that the course set out to provide them with. It gives an overall picture or snapshot of what the student has learned. Summative assessment can come at the end of a course (for example through writing a dissertation), or it can be carried out on a *continuous* basis during the programme (for example through the gradual building up of a portfolio). As such, continuous summative assessment can at the same time have a formative function.

Validity and reliability of assessment

Validity of assessment refers to the extent to which an assessment task satisfactorily assesses the content that is supposed to be assessed. There are several elements to this: content validity (does the content of the assessment appropriately match up to the content of the course?); construct validity (has the assessment been presented and constructed in such a way that it is understood and achievable?); predictive validity (will the assessment provide sufficient information regarding student competence and performance to stakeholders such as future employers?); and face validity (does the assessment measure what was intended?).

Reliability of assessment refers to the consistency and rigour of the assessment process. To ensure that an assessment task is reliable, it needs to be demonstrated as being fair. Irrespective of where the assessment is carried out or who will mark it (for example), the assessment decision should always be consistent. Reliability of assessment, therefore, is all about removing bias or subjectivity from the assessment process so that grading is consistent through the use of predetermined and public assessment criteria, results are checked through second marking and external examination, and so forth.

Feedback

The provision of any form of assessment is, arguably, a waste of time and effort if feedback is not going to be given. Feedback should be considered an essential part of the assessment process, whatever mode of assessment is being employed. Feedback will be qualitatively different depending on the type of assessment being undertaken: a question-and-answer session in the classroom (informal formative assessment) will generate feedback that is quite different from the kind of feedback that will be provided for an essay or report (formal summative assessment).

A number of criteria should always be borne in mind when planning for and delivering feedback. Feedback should be: clear and unambiguous (where necessary it should refer to assessment tasks and learning outcomes); specific (particular issues or topics should be commented on for either praise or corrective work); supportive and developmental (of particular importance when working with non-traditional students); timely (if there is a delay in giving feedback the student may have 'moved on' and the value of the feedback may be lessened); and understood and delivered in an appropriate manner (for example, giving feedback on an essay should take place in a quiet and supportive environment).

REFLECTIVE TASK

REFLECTIVE TASK

The preceding discussion demonstrates quite clearly that the key theories and principles that under-pin assessment practice in the FE sector are to be found in HE as well. These issues are familiar components of teacher-training programmes within the lifelong learning sector more generally and are likely to be familiar to people as they read this book. Before reading on, take the time to reflect on how moving to teach within HE in FE provision might lead to different working practices, or even different perspectives, on some of the themes that have been discussed here. For example, will the way you approach your marking change? Will you have to give different kinds of feedback, or design new kinds of formative assessment activities? Will you need to provide study skills support as part of your assessment and feedback practice?

These sorts of questions will be explored in more depth when we begin our analysis of current debates in HE assessment practice, but a few typical examples of the kinds of issues reported by HE in FE lecturers might help to set the scene for this debate:

- For some lecturers, giving feedback relating to academic writing and referencing con-stitutes a challenge. Writing and referencing are important academic skills that at times can require significant development.
- It can be difficult to establish and maintain a balance between providing support and guidance for HE in FE students on the one hand, and developing independent, auton-omous study skills on the other. This is of particular importance when considering students on a foundation degree who will be studying for their top-up degree at a uni-versity rather than in college.
- Some lecturers may not have designed their own summative assessment activities before moving into HE in FE teaching.
- HE in FE lecturers will need to work with assessment criteria from the university or uni-versities that accredit the programmes on which they teach. These can be difficult to 'get to know' in the first instance.
- Marking scales in HE are quite different from those used in FE. A mark that is given to an undergraduate piece of work is not a percentage in the strictest sense. That is to say, giving an essay a mark of 64 does not mean that the student got 64 per cent of the answer 'right'. Instead, the mark of 64 is a numerical representation of the fact that the essay has been graded as being in the upper second class band, just below the half-way point. Similarly, a very good essay might receive a mark of 80 or even 85, which indicates a first class mark – but work like this is very rare and such high marks are only rarely used. It can be difficult to explain to a student that a mark of 64 is actu-ally a good mark – which it is!

As we can see, therefore, there are lots of issues to discuss when considering HE in FE assess-ment practices. We shall now turn to a discussion of topics that can be seen as being relevant to HE in FE lecturers, and which are represented in current research and policy literature.

Current debates in HE assessment practice

We have selected the following five areas as representative of current debates in HE assessment practice. Each of these will be explored in terms of their relevance to assessment practices in HE in FE, and full citations for the research or policy literature that is referred to can be found at the end of this chapter. The five topics are:

1. Employability skills and transferable skills.
2. Marking to the outcomes or a holistic judgement?
3. Assessment design as a tool to change patterns of student engagement.
4. Feedback and feedforward.
5. Encouraging student autonomy.

Employability skills and transferable skills

It does not take long for even the newest FE lecturer to come up against the (sometimes) controversial topics of basic and key or functional skills (the exact terminology keeps changing – by the time this book is published, it might have changed again). Skills such as literacy and numeracy are present across the FE curriculum in one form or another and are seen as being important by employers, policy makers and curriculum bodies alike. The 'key skills debate' is not a feature of the HE curriculum in quite the same way, although module specifications tend to include 'transferable' or 'generic' skills (whatever they might be – there is a critical scholarly debate on this subject), but a parallel can be found in the 'employability agenda' that is an increasingly common feature of the HE curriculum and, by extension, of the HE in FE curriculum as well.

Employability is the term used to gather together and describe those skills or attributes that employers expect graduates from university-level courses to possess. One way in which employability can be defined is through thinking about the skills that employers look for:

- Creativity.
- Flexibility.
- Willingness to learn.
- Autonomy.
- Working in a team.
- Ability to manage others.
- Ability to work under pressure.
- Good oral communication.
- Good written communication.
- Numeracy.
- Attention to detail.
- Good time management skills.
- Ability to make decisions.
- Ability to plan and organise.

(Thomas and Jones, 2007, page 22)

A more holistic approach proposed by Yorke (2008, page 11) defines employability as:

> *a set of achievements – skills, understandings and personal attributes – that makes graduates more likely to gain employment and be successful in their chosen occupations, which benefits themselves, the workforce, the community and the economy.*

However, it is important to reflect on the fact that such debates tend to focus on the experience of full-time undergraduates, rather than the kinds of students who study HE in FE. HE in FE students tend to study on part-time courses, often while working on either a part-time or full-time basis and often (though by no means always) study courses that are directly linked to particular professional, technical or other occupational roles. Foundation degrees in particular, one might argue, are based on curricula that by definition are all about employability (not least as they are invariably designed in consultation with employers, professional bodies and such like).

As such, individual modules as well as curricula are expected to address employability issues. Some of these will be more or less relevant to HE in FE students. For example: full-time students would clearly benefit from work placement or volunteering opportunities if these contributed to their wider learning during their programme of studies. For part-time students, though, such requirements may be either not necessary (as they are already in work and as such they have already gained experience of the workplace) or too difficult to manage (as part-time students will have work, family and other commitments, making a placement highly impractical). The opportunity to draw on practical workplace experiences as part of an assignment task, however, would be highly beneficial to part-time students. Such work-based assignments carry high levels of authenticity and hence validity. And finally, using a personal development plan (PDP) to reflect on learning and consider how it helps develop particular skills that would be useful for future employment would be of use to all students, whatever their status.

At the same time, it is important to note that the very notion of employability skills is somewhat controversial and that for some lecturers in HE, embedding employability raises awkward questions. This is not simply a reflection of the views of a minority who might argue that the 'purpose' of HE is not about employability and that university lecturers should focus solely on teaching 'their subject' without worrying about employability (or, indeed, any other wider benefits of engaging in HE). Rather, the questions raised are more to do with how the individual student is positioned within the employability debate. Within discourses of employability, transferable skills and lifelong learning more generally, the onus is always on the individual: if you want to get a good job, you need the correct employability skills, and if you do not have them, you need to enrol on another programme of study (this is a simplification, it should be noted, of a much more complex and nuanced argument). But the extent to which employers should – or should not – help with both the initial and ongoing training and development of employees is lost sight of. And employability should not be conflated with employment. Even if a number of graduates do indeed possess all of the employability skills that employers say that they want, it does not follow that they will all step into 'graduate jobs'. Local and regional economic factors, personal and familial circumstances and simple necessity ('I need to be earning in order to pay my fees') all influence the kinds of jobs that people take upon leaving a HE course. So yes, HE is in part about getting a job – perhaps even a 'better' one (which might not be the same as a more highly paid one). But there is still much more to HE than simply collecting a series of transferable skills.

Marking to the outcomes or a holistic judgement?

It goes without saying that making the right assessment decision is of the upmost importance across both the FE and HE sectors. The award of certificates or diplomas – perhaps in turn leading to the award of a professional license or status – can have profound implications for the future trajectories of our students. The 'right result' can open doors to higher levels of study, to employment, or to promotion in the workplace. As such, it is of vital importance that the assessment decisions that lead to awards such as these are correct, robust and capable of standing up to external scrutiny.

In universities as well as in colleges, a number of processes and resources have been developed over time in order to ensure that assessment systems are both valid and reliable (as discussed above). Although the particular terminology used may vary somewhat from institution to institution, the most common systems in HE (which behave in a manner similar to their FE counterparts) include:

1. Marking criteria that provide grade descriptors for assessed work at different levels (NQF levels 4, 5 and 6 for undergraduates, level 7 for masters and level 8 for doctoral work). Typically these will provide guidance as to structure, argument, and use of resources and appropriate academic conventions that can help the assessor decide what grade or classification a piece of work should receive.
2. Module documentation that includes learning outcomes, assessment tasks and indicative content. A single module might contain more than one assessment task, but all the tasks for a module must always cover all of the learning outcomes.
3. Meetings between first and second markers, and between internal markers and external examiners provide further opportunities for checking the marks that have been given and ensuring a consistent approach. Second markers, or 'moderators', and external examiners will usually receive a sample of work from the first marker (with the exception of failed work and work awarded a first class mark, which are normally always moderated).

At first look, therefore, it would seem to be the case that a typical assessment process might go like this: the first marker reads the assignment, and then refers to the module documentation in order to ensure sufficient coverage of the module content in the assignment. Once the marker is satisfied that the module outcomes have been met, they would then turn to the marking criteria in order to establish the grade that the assignment will be given.

However, research would seem to indicate that things are not quite so straightforward. According to research by Kathryn Ecclestone published over a decade ago (which explored assessment practices on a HE in FE programme across a network of FE colleges), the use of guidelines, criteria and the like are in fact complex processes and not at all straightforward. In her research, Ecclestone found that after moderation, the essays that had been marked by 'experts' (that is, more experienced staff) were adjusted more frequently than the essays that had been marked by 'novices' (Ecclestone, 2001). Other complexities that emerged from her research included the following:

- Experts in a particular topic were more likely to notice – or to notice a lack of – 'critical analysis' in assignments and grade the work accordingly.
- Staff use criteria and guidelines in very variable ways. 'Experts' use them less often than 'novices', who tend to use them as a way of learning about assessment practice. Some 'experts' do not use them at all.
- The assessment decisions of 'experts' need to be moderated as frequently as the decisions of 'novices'.

Ten years later, a paper written by Sue Bloxham, Peter Boyd and Susan Orr would seem to indicate that these complexities are still a common feature of academic life in the HE sector. For their research, Bloxham et al. asked university assessors to take part in a series of 'thinking aloud' assessment meetings in order to explore how assessment decisions were being made (Bloxham et al., 2011). They found that:

- lecturers tended to make initial holistic judgements about assignments, and then used criteria and marking schemes in order to refine this decision. For example: a lecturer might decide that an assignment was worth a 2:2, and then use the guidelines to decide the exact mark (which might range from 50 to 59);
- most lecturers only use guidelines and criteria after making an initial judgement, usually as a way of justifying their decisions – some do not use them at all;
- some lecturers expressed disagreement with the criteria and guidelines that they were being asked to use, and this made a difference to the assessment decisions that they made.

Marking students' work would seem to be more complicated than merely ticking off the different outcomes that an assignment is supposed to cover. Over time, lecturers develop their own understandings of and approaches to assessment as an aspect of their wider professional learning and experience (Eraut, 1995). Criteria and guidelines are important, but so are the conversations that take place around them and the meetings between markers that allow an understanding of assessment to be developed and debated. Learning to assess in HE in FE, therefore, requires more than just a set of published outcomes and guidelines: it requires opportunities for meaningful discussions between HE in FE staff, and with staff from the relevant HE institution. Instead of being left to work in relative isolation, HE in FE managers need to allow HE in FE teaching staff the time and space needed for collaborative, scholarly discussions about how assessment works.

Assessment design as a tool to change patterns of student engagement

Lecturers in both colleges and universities tend to want the same things from their students: a good level of motivation, a willingness to engage, regular attendance and a desire to move beyond surface learning and to engage in deep learning instead. As such, it can be difficult for lecturers (and here we speak from experience) when, at the end of a seminar, one or more of the students in attendance ask: 'is this going to be part of our assessment?' Whether we like it or not, we will invariably encounter students who appear to focus solely on the assessment at the end of the module or programme. By this we mean to draw attention to that element of student behaviour that seems almost to block out any aspect of the learning experience that does not have a direct relevance to the assignment. Some students will miss classes that they do not perceive as relevant to the assessment, or be reluctant to engage in formative assessment strategies that do not contribute to their final grades or awards. It can be difficult for lecturers to appreciate that not all of their students share their motivation for the subject. Little wonder, then, that 'teaching to the test' has become a common aspect of pedagogic activity in both further and HE.

Such an instrumental or strategic approach to studying is in some senses, perhaps, understandable and justifiable. Students often have other, legitimate, demands on their time that can distract them from their studies. This is particularly the case with part-time and non-traditional students – the very definition of the HE in FE student. If you have a full-time job or have to provide care to a relative, for example, it can be easy for your studies to be affected. Anything that does not appear relevant might therefore be questioned or challenged. At the same time, there are good academic reasons why HE in FE lecturers (or, indeed, any lecturers working with student groups such as these) should find ways to encourage students to engage with the curriculum as fully as possible. Put simply, as lecturers we know that those students who do engage, who do take on a deep as opposed to a surface approach to their students, will get more from the process (and not just in terms of grades or certificates). The careful design of assessment strategies can be one way of encouraging this.

RESEARCH FOCUS RESEARCH FOCUS **RESEARCH** FOCUS RESEARCH FOCUS

Expanding assessment methods and moments

In an article published in 2012, Jennifer Frost, Genevieve du Pont and Ian Brailsford describe and analyse the introduction of a new form of *continuous assessment* within a module being studied by history students at a university. Their starting point for this new assessment model was a concern over irregular attendance by students and the impact that this was having on their learning. The authors wanted to find ways of encouraging regular tutorial attendance and also encouraging more regular and systematic engagement with the course being studied.

Frost et al. decided to introduce weekly continuous assessment tasks, which they called 'tutorial assignments' because they were based on work done in that week's tutorial session. Students would have to write a short essay-style assignment each week throughout the ten-week module. These were designed to be developmental and to move the students away from merely descriptive writing towards more analytical writing. In this way it was hoped that by the time that the students began their final assignments, their work would be of a higher quality. Each tutorial assignment counted towards the student's final mark so as to further encourage completion, although the end project remained the most substantial assessment component.

Over the course of the module, Frost et al. found that the tutorial assignments were highly effective. Students engaged with them and reported that they were a useful tool for learning (that is, they had a formative function as well as contributing to end grades). The grades received in the end-of-module assignments were higher than had been the case in the previous year. The negative consequences of this innovation did not impact on the students, however, but on the staff, who reported that the time taken to administer, assess and give feedback to the tutorial assignments was rather greater than had been anticipated.

This research was conducted in a university but is immediately applicable to HE in FE contexts as well. It is all too easy for opportunities for formative assessment and, hence, deep learning to be lost sight of, particularly among part-time students. Such a use of continuous summative assessment provides one method by which more regular engagement can be encouraged. It is straightforward for new assessment tasks to be designed and accredited within university curricula and if carefully designed need not be unduly burdensome on the lecturer.

Feedback and feedforward

As lecturers in colleges and/or universities, we give feedback to our students in all kinds of ways. Just as there are many different ways of assessing our students – formal and informal, formative and summative – so there is a corresponding variety of methods that we can employ in order to give students feedback. Feedback can be written down, or spoken out loud. It is often provided on a one-to-one basis, but can also be given on a shared or group basis. Feedback can be a developmental tool, and it can provide an analysis of what a student has achieved.

There are a number of key themes to keep in mind when giving feedback, irrespective of the educational sector in question. These can be summarised as follows (Tummons, 2011):

- **Feedback should be clear and unambiguous.** Feedback needs to be straightforward and written in everyday language, and if we do need to use more specialised language (technical terms, for example), we need to ensure firstly that the student understands what the words used actually mean, and secondly that the student understands what actions (as appropriate) are needed to develop or improve their performance.

- **Feedback should be specific.** It is all too common for students to read comments on their feedback sheets such as 'this section is too general', or 'you have failed to answer the question'. But students need to know *in what way* an essay is 'too general' and *exactly* what they need to do to 'answer the question'. Good feedback should therefore refer explicitly to the assignment task, criteria or learning outcomes that are at hand. This is not to say that general comments are unwelcome, as they do provide a useful way of starting a discussion with the student. But such general comments need to be followed by more specific and constructive advice.

- **Feedback should be supportive, formative and developmental.** Good feedback should allow the student to build on their past successes and at the same time move away from errors in understanding or mistakes in technical execution. It is all too easy to reduce feedback to a simple list of the actions necessary to ensure a pass (an 'instrumental' approach to feedback) without properly explaining why these steps are necessary as part of the broader learning experience. Similarly, it is easy to write 'good' in the margins of a written paper (and even easier just to put a tick) with no explanation of what in particular has been done well. Such a cursory approach diminishes the potential for feedback, and hence assessment, to act as a tool for learning.

- **Feedback should be timely.** For feedback to be effective, it needs to come as quickly as possible after the assessment activity itself. The exact timing of feedback will depend on several factors: the time it takes for the lecturer to mark the work; the availability of both lecturer and student to meet, if required; whether or not an assessment needs to be second marked (see above); and the nature of the assess-ment itself (informal formative assessment of, for example, a class-based activity can be instantaneous, whereas formal formative assessment may require a lengthy marking process). Immediate or near-immediate feedback will be most useful to the student. It is worth noting that university departments often set guidelines as to how quickly students can expect feedback on their work.

- **Spoken feedback should be delivered in an appropriate environment.** If feedback is pro-vided in written form only, the 'where' of the feedback is less important than the 'when'. But if spoken feedback is required, place as well as time needs to be considered. Giving feedback on a written assignment need not take place in the room where the taught ses-sions are held: a coffee bar may be preferable if both student and lecturer agree that this more informal atmosphere is appropriate. Other students may prefer a more quiet and secluded setting, such as a seminar room, library workspace or staff room. In all such situations, lecturers should take the time to check that the student is comfortable: if not, consider rearranging the tutorial session.

Although the principles and practice of feedback are well established throughout both the FE and HE sectors, it continues nonetheless to form a focus for research and criti-cal inquiry. Perhaps the most important trend to emerge in recent years in HE-focused teaching and learning literature is the concept of *feedforward* (Price et al., 2010). Feed-forward is the term used to focus on the *developmental* aspects of the assessment pro-cess. Criticisms of standard university feedback processes tend to focus on the fact that much feedback appears to be more-or-less ignored by students, and that there is too much focus on what the student has just done rather than what the student might do next time. Instead, it is argued that feed*forward* as well as feed*back* is needed in order to provide students with explicit guidance as to how to improve the quality of their work in the future.

Encouraging student autonomy

What is 'student autonomy'? It is a term that is widely used, often alongside other expressions such as 'independent learners' or 'critical thinking', which pop up in textbooks, student handbooks and external examiners' reports. Within the HE sector, there is an ongoing, and sometimes fractious, conversation regarding 'student autonomy' – what it might mean and how it might be achieved.

One of the espoused aims of the HE sector – whatever the subject matter might be – is to help students become critical, thoughtful and well-informed commentators on and participants in the world around them (which might relate to working environment, or to society more generally). It is perhaps unfashionable to say so – in a time of managerialism, league tables, employability agendas, fees and marketing – but the vast majority of university lecturers want their students to do well in their subject, to appreciate the learning of that subject on its own terms and to be willing to do the work that is needed in order to learn. In this context, one of the developmental aspects of student learning that lecturers expect to see is an increased level of autonomy. Put simply, lecturers expect students to get better at working 'on their own' as their studies progress. This is not to say that lecturers expect to spend less actual time with final year students as opposed to new students: but they do expect the nature of that time to change, to be less about helping students learn how to learn and more about a deep and thorough exploration of the curriculum.

This gradual transition towards student autonomy might make sense in the context of mainstream full-time undergraduate provision, but is rendered more complicated when we consider the much more diverse nature of HE in FE provision. The needs of students who are part-time, who do not hold standard entry qualifications, who have been away from formal education for some time and who need to work and look after their families, are clearly quite difference from the needs of full-time undergraduates. And in turn, expectations of student autonomy will also be different. A part-time top-up student cannot – and should not – be expected to engage in autonomous learning in the same manner or through the provision of the same curriculum as a full-time undergraduate. If we accept that the wider learning, teaching and assessment of non-traditional students is understood as being qualitatively different to that of traditional students, we should, therefore, also accept that student autonomy will be different in HE in FE.

So how can assessment help us engage deeper and more autonomous approaches to learning among our students? One common approach is to consider how students learn how to do assessment, not only in terms such as academic writing skills ('how to construct an essay'), but also in terms of understanding how the process works so that students are best able to understand and then meet their assignment requirements. Such approaches have been shown to be effective in universities (Rust et al., 2003). More importantly – from the point of view of the HE in FE practitioner – they have also been shown to be effective in the transition from FE to HE.

RESEARCH FOCUS RESEARCH FOCUS **RESEARCH** FOCUS RESEARCH FOCUS

Helping FE students understand HE assessment criteria

In a research paper published in 2009, Anna Jessen and James Elander describe and analyse research that they conducted in order to explore ways by which FE students might better make the transition to

(Continued)

(Continued)

HE through a focus on assessment. If the students had a better understanding of assessment criteria, they argued, they would be more likely to engage in deep as opposed to surface learning. Through comparing students who had received specific guidance and support in working with HE criteria with students who had not, they found that the students who received additional support demonstrated a more critical and sophisticated perspective on essay writing, even though their levels of confidence were reduced. This research demonstrates that although it might be difficult in the short term for students to have to come to know about new ways of writing when entering HE because their confidence may be affected, they nonetheless acquired more realistic understandings of essay writing in HE.

A SUMMARY OF KEY POINTS

During this chapter, we have looked at the following key issues:
➢ The principles and practices of assessment are well established and are common across both the FE and HE sectors.
➢ Assessment in HE, and in HE in FE, continues nonetheless to be controversial, and to be a focus for research and inquiry. In some areas in particular – employability, the use of outcomes and criteria, student engagement, feedback and student autonomy – debate is lively and not always straightforwardly conclusive.

Assessment practice in HE is well established, carefully audited, and widely recognised as being fit for purpose: stakeholders have confidence in the assessment decisions that are made and hence in the certificates and awards that our students receive. At the same time, it is an area for speculation, inquiry and reflection. It should not be treated as unproblematic. We hope that the (necessarily brief) discussions that have been presented here provide a first step into a critical reflection on assessment in HE that will be of value to the HE in FE lecturer.

Branching options
Reflection

As you look back over this chapter, think about which of the arguments and debates around assessment seem the most convincing, as well as those which seem weaker or less relevant to your own context. Talk with colleagues or with students and compare your views. How might your assessment practice address some of the complexities alluded to in this chapter?

Analysis

At the beginning of this chapter you were presented with well-established definitions of key assessment principles such as validity and reliability. Have your ideas changed as you have read this chapter? If so, how or why have they changed? How can an understanding of the problematic aspects of assessment and its implications for your students contribute to your own professional knowledge or challenge your professional practice?

Research

Assessment is a rich and complex topic: the outcomes of assessment (certificates, diplomas and degrees) are important and both need and deserve to be critically understood. The references that appear below are all recommended for further study. The kind of research done by Ecclestone and by Jessen and Elander is of particular relevance in part due to their FE focus and in part due to the fact that they might inform your own responses to assessment in HE in FE contexts.

REFERENCES REFERENCES REFERENCES

Bloxham, S., Boyd, P. and Orr, S. (2011) Mark my words: the role of assessment criteria in UK higher education grading practices, *Studies in Higher Education,* 36(6): 655–70.

Ecclestone, K. (2001) 'I know a 2:1 when I see it': understanding criteria for degree classifications in franchised university programmes, *Journal of Further and Higher Education,* 25(3): 301–13.

Eraut, M. (1995) *Developing Professional Knowledge and Competence*. London: Routledge.

Frost, J., de Pont, G. and Brailsford, I. (2012) Expanding assessment methods and moments in history, *Studies in Higher Education,* 37(3): 293–304.

Price, M., Handley, K., Millar, J. and O'Donovan, B. (2010) Feedback: all that effort, but what is the effect? *Assessment and Evaluation in Higher Education,* 35(3): 277–89.

Rust, C., Price, M. and O'Donovan, B. (2003) Improving students' learning by developing their understanding of assessment criteria and processes, *Assessment and Evaluation in Higher Education,* 28(1): 147–64.

Thomas, L. and Jones, R. (2007) *Embedding Employability in the Context of Widening Participation*. York: Higher Education Academy.

Tummons, J. (2011) *Assessing Learning in the Lifelong Learning Sector*. Third edition Exeter: Learning Matters.

Yorke, M. (2008) *Employability and Higher Education: What It is – What It is Not* (2nd edition). York: Higher Education Academy.

7

Research and scholarship in HE in FE

By the end of this chapter you will be able to:

- contextualise the place of research and scholarly activity within HE in FE provision;
- evaluate differing definitions of scholarly activity;
- critically reflect on your own position in relation to research and scholarly activity.

Introduction: setting the scene for research and scholarship

What are the 'big' differences that can be found when comparing teaching FE to teaching HE? At one time, the most recognisable or conspicuous difference – and certainly one that would be recognised by society at large – might have been to do with the subject matter or the content of the courses being compared. Some subject areas would straightforwardly be seen as belonging in a university. These would be theoretical, linked to employment in the professions, and seen as being 'harder'. They would be taught by acknowledged experts, who would base their teaching on enormous quantities of reading and research. They would also be seen as being more prestigious. And all of this would be linked to academic performance: if you 'got the grades' in your exams when you were 16, then you would go to sixth form college and then to university, often quite far away from home. If you didn't get the grades, you would go to your local FE college and 'get a trade' – and there would be little or no opportunities for a university education in the future.

However, none of this really applies any more (which is a good thing!). To a significant degree this is due to the expansion of university provision during the last 50 years or so. The first wave of expansion came in the 1960s when the so-called 'plate glass' universities were established (they were called this because of the architectural style of many of their campuses). They were built in different parts of the country where there were no 'local' universities (Lancaster, Sussex, York and Warwick, for example) and were designed to encourage local economic growth as well as facilitate an expansion of university provision. So in a way, these universities made up the 'widening participation' agenda of the time. These days, the universities of the 1960s are all classified as 'research intensive'. They define themselves in terms of the excellent quality of their research – according to the positions that they obtain in relevant league tables and through membership of what might be called university groups or associations that are focused on research. The Universities of Warwick and York are both members of the 'Russell Group' of research-intensive universities (the group is named after the hotel in London where representatives from these universities first met and established their group). The universities of Lancaster and Sussex are members of the '1994 Group' of research-intensive universities (which is perceived – whether rightly or wrongly is another matter – as being a bit less prestigious than the Russell Group).

The next significant wave of university expansion – which is where the HE in FE agenda that is at the heart of this book needs to be understood – came 20 years ago when the polytechnics (as they were then called) were converted into universities. The polytechnics (many of which had roots that went back to the Mechanics Institutes of the Victorian period) had traditionally delivered technical and professional curricula as opposed to the academic curricula of the universities. It was argued that if all of these HE institutions became universities, this divide might be bridged. In fact, the universities that used to be polytechnics (such as Huddersfield and Teesside), together with newer universities that have been established since 1992 (such as Lincoln) are still classified differently within the HE world. They tend to be referred to – and to refer to themselves – as 'teaching universities', distinct from the older 'research-intensive' universities. This is not to say that these newer universities do not engage in research in the ways that the older ones do. But research tends to be carried out by a smaller proportion of staff, and tends as a result to make up less of the university's income. Within these 'teaching universities', some staff are research active, publishing in academic journals and bidding for research grants, while others are not. The research done in these universities is of a comparable 'quality' (whatever that might mean), but there is, simply put, a bit less of it. This is not to say that staff in these universities do not engage in wider scholarly activity such as studying for higher degrees, attending conferences and such like. But a distinction is drawn between 'research' and between 'scholarly activity', which are not (as shall be discussed below) quite the same thing. Some of these newer universities, such as Bath Spa, Wolverhampton and Middlesex, are affiliated to the 'million plus' university think-tank, which promotes wider access to university education.

But why is any of this relevant or important to a discussion of research and scholarship in HE in FE? The answer lies in the diversity of research and scholarly activity that can be seen across a university sector that is in itself increasingly diverse. At some universities, there is an expectation that everyone who works there as a lecturer should be doing research and then writing up and publishing their findings. At other universities, there is an aspiration rather than an expectation that lecturers will research and publish, but it is in no way a requirement. But they will all engage in wider scholarly activity. Moreover, what 'counts' as research or as scholarship will vary according to the curriculum area or body of knowledge being discussed. The expansion of university provision over the last 20 years has seen the growth of new areas of curriculum provision within HE ranging from nursing to sports science and on to computer games design. What gets defined as a 'university subject' has changed a lot – and will continue to do so – and consequently, what counts as research and scholarship has changed as well. The expansion of HE in FE provision over the last 20 years is in a way simply another element of this wider expansion of HE. As such, it seems right to consider how research and scholarship (which despite ongoing arguments about what these mean and who might be involved in them are seen as defining characteristics of university-level provision) might be made sense of within FE colleges where HE programmes are delivered, and by FE staff who also teach on HE programmes.

REFLECTIVE TASK

What do 'research' and 'scholarly activity' mean to you?

Take some time to note down what you consider 'research' and 'scholarly activity' to mean and to imply for the working life of the HE in FE lecturer. What kinds of activities do you think that you are

(Continued)

(Continued)

already engaged with that might count as research and scholarly activity, and what kinds of activities do you aspire to take part in in the future? It may be the case that there are various barriers or enablers around you that you will need to take notice of: these might relate to your individual working conditions or to your contractual status, or to the institution in which you work. If you are teaching on HE programmes in partnership with a university, does this HE partner have anything to say on the subject of research and scholarly activity?

Defining research and scholarly activity

Different universities define 'research' and 'scholarly activity' in different ways, usually as an aspect of the contractual agreements that are in place relating to the workloads of lecturing staff. At some institutions, a range or variety of activities might be described as being examples of 'research and scholarly activity' (here deliberately joined together to make a single category) and which staff would be expected to engage with during research and scholarly activity (RSA) time – as distinct from the time they would spend teaching. In such situations, RSA might include writing a conference paper, applying for funding from a research council, studying towards a doctorate (a significant number of lecturers in new universities in particular study for a doctorate) or writing a textbook. These activities are in themselves all quite distinct and represent different stages of the research process. Writing a conference paper requires the author to have done some research beforehand. Applying for funding is not research in itself, but the research plans that such applications require need to be of a high quality and demand significant expertise, and often prior experience of successful research as well. Studying for a doctorate can be seen at one level as a form of apprenticeship, after which the student will be able to enter the community of educational research. And writing a textbook may not in itself require any research to be done, but does require a significant quantity of reading and a critical understanding of that reading that takes time and effort.

In practice, it would appear to be the case that lecturing staff themselves draw distinctions between these different activities in just the same way that universities, at an institutional level, do. For example, from the point of view of the research league tables that all universities look to, writing an article for an academic journal 'counts' as research – but writing a textbook does not. The establishment of a community of doctoral-level students is seen as helping to establish a 'culture of research' within a university department, but in itself is not valued as highly – for the purposes of the evaluation of research activities within the HE sector – as scholarly outputs such as articles and successful bids for research money. By contrast, a culture of scholarly activity is taken for granted within universities. So what might these distinct terms actually mean?

A definition of research

What is research? For the purposes of this discussion, we shall define research as a process of systematic investigation, carefully planned, thought through and executed, in order to find out the answers to particular research questions. Through carrying out this research work and through establishing answers to the questions that we are interested in, new knowledge and/or new understanding will always be created. Research can be carried out in a number of different ways (which are outside the scope of this book, but there are many textbooks on research method and methodology to help you understand them), and can be used to investigate educational issues or problems at very local, institutional or national and international levels. Whatever the scale or scope of the research, the fundamental processes of research always stay the same (Tummons and Duckworth, 2012).

A definition of scholarly activity

What is scholarly activity? For the purposes of this discussion, we shall define scholarly activity as the process of systematic reading, evaluation and discussion that allows the lecturer to establish a thorough, critical and up-to-date understanding of their specialism or curriculum interest. In this way, they become 'expert' in the subject area being taught. Scholarly activity is not about generating new knowledge in the way that research it, but it is about more than simply reading up on a subject before teaching it to a group of students – a phenomenon referred to as *reading to teach* (Feather, 2012a). As we have already seen, staff in newer universities in particular are not always expected to engage in research (the extent to which this is desirable is another matter, however). But staff in newer universities are expected to engage in scholarship – to be thoroughly versed in the subjects that they teach, to be up to date in their reading and aware of current trends of thought and practice in their field. Indeed, such a level of conspicuous expertise is – arguably – a defining quality of the university lecturer from the point of view of the students themselves.

From research to teaching, via scholarship

When discussing the work of university lecturers, the two activities of 'research' and 'teaching' have over time tended to be separated and valued differently. One way of bringing these two activities together has been through the notion of scholarship as the bridge between research and teaching. That is to say, if research is all about generating new knowledge and teaching is all about reinterpreting and delivering knowledge in the classroom or workshop, scholarship is the practice of engaging with that knowledge in a critical and thorough manner. Instead of creating a divide between the work of research and the work of teaching, the broader notion of scholarship might be seen as being more inclusive, as acknowledging that not everyone involved in HE will do research but will nonetheless engage with their subject specialism in a rigorous, critical and intellectually curious manner.

Research and scholarly activity in FE colleges: the experience and culture of HE in FE

At some point, of course, we actually need to consider the extent to which research and scholarly activity is either needed or wanted in HE in FE. Asking whether research and scholarship should actually 'be' in FE colleges where HE courses are delivered might seem to be a heretical question to ask, but it is an important one to consider. HE in FE is different to 'mainstream' HE (whatever that might be). It is not a subset or subsection of mainstream HE provision; nor should it be simplistically defined as 'outreach' or 'extramural' provision. Rather, it should be seen as a particular kind of provision in its own right: distinctive, with its own rules, norms and culture (Parry and Thompson, 2002).

Indeed, it might be argued that even within the confines of the FE college, HE provision is complex. Provision varies from foundation degrees (which may be delivered in conjunction with a university or may be awarded by the college itself) through to top-up degrees, and from qualifications for nursery staff to qualifications for chartered accountants. Allowing for this complex landscape, some common themes can be discerned that can be seen as being relevant to a discussion about the establishment of a culture of research and scholarship in HE in FE. There are three main themes to consider. First, we shall consider those factors that might be seen as being barriers to the establishment of such cultures. Second, we shall consider those factors that might be seen as being the benefits of HE in FE provision from the point of view of staff who might wish to engage in research. And third, we shall consider the broader issue of whether research and scholarship is in itself desirable in HE in FE cultures.

Barriers to research and scholarship in HE in FE

There has been a considerable expansion of research into HE in FE provision more generally over recent years, and a number of important publications have explored research and scholarship in HE in FE from the point of view of both the institution and the individuals who work in them.

Institutional and organisational barriers to research and scholarship in HE in FE

The first point to note is that FE colleges do not primarily position themselves as engaging in research: it is, simply put, not something that the vast majority of colleges set out to do, although a small number of colleges have over time devoted resources to research work (Hillier and Thompson, 2005). Universities have been doing research for decades – centuries, in some cases. It is simply unrealistic to assume that at an institutional level, colleges should be able to catch up. However, notwithstanding the position that FE colleges occupy, it can also be argued that should staff wish to embark upon research and scholarship, there are cultural reasons that hinder this process that go beyond simply defining the college as 'not a place for research'. The broader working conditions that impact on all college staff have implications for HE in FE as well (Gleeson et al., 2005; Spenceley, 2006).

At the centre of this debate is the culture or nature of the FE sector. Contemporary FE cultures are characterised by performativity and managerialism, by a culture that seeks to audit and measure everything that happens (Avis, 2005; Shain and Gleeson, 1999). Over the last 20 years or so, working conditions have changed considerably in colleges: management cultures have reduced the autonomy of lecturers; there have been increases in the number of working hours that college lecturers are expected to be teaching; there has been an expansion of the kinds of duties that lecturers are expected to perform; and finally, the pace of curriculum change within the sector has grown. In such working environments as these, there is barely enough time to draw breath, never mind to engage in research and scholarship. HE in FE staff do find that there is enough time to stay 'one step ahead' of their students, but there is not much more time than this. Many HE in FE staff teach across other sectors of the 14–19 curriculum as well, often on multiple programmes and for more than one examining or awarding body. Planning for teaching across multiple programmes and managing the bureaucratic requirements of several different awarding bodies is complex and time-consuming work.

Individual and personal barriers to research and scholarship in HE in FE

A further complex factor emerges when we consider the extent to which lecturers working in FE colleges actually wish to conduct research or to engage in the scholarship of their subject specialism beyond the immediate requirements of the curricula that they teach. Some researchers have argued that teachers in FE do not identify themselves in terms of their subject specialism, but in terms of their teaching. FE teachers often teach across more than one specialist area, reflecting their own varied professional or occupational backgrounds and their often similarly varied professional or post-compulsory qualifications (Young, 2002). FE staff tend to position themselves in relation to their expertise as teachers rather than as scholars – if indeed they do in fact identify themselves as teachers in the first place: for many staff in FE, it is their technical, craft or occupational identity rather than their identity as an educator that dominates (Orr and Simmons, 2010). And for those FE lecturers who do foreground their role as teachers, this is often in terms of being experts in teaching rather than experts in a particular specialism, reflecting the changes to working cultures in FE over recent years that have helped position the individual lecturer as a 'multi-skilled learning professional', able to pick up and 'deliver' a curriculum at short notice as the market demands (Wilson and Wilson, 2011).

For the college lecturer who does wish to engage in research and scholarship, the same pressures of time and workload combine with other factors to erect further barriers. The practicalities of research take time, as does the level of reading that scholarship requires. Moreover, any spare time that is available might be lost to formal – and sometimes compulsory – continuing professional development (CPD). Over recent years, the 'professionalisation' agenda in FE has led to changes in CPD provision, neatly encapsulated by the requirements for all college staff to undertake compulsory CPD as an element of qualified teacher learning and skills (QTLS) professional formation and Institute for Learning (IfL) membership. But formal CPD activities (staff training days being the most obvious format) tend to be dominated by procedural and administrative content, leaving little time for academic discussion or speculation, let alone for learning about how to conduct research that is robust and ethically sound.

Positioning research and scholarship in HE in FE

Amidst these individual and organisational difficulties, it might seem that research and scholarship is very far from the top of the 'jobs to do' list of the typical HE in FE lecturer. And this is hardly surprising, allowing for the workplace culture of FE (bureaucratic and burdensome at best, anti-intellectual at worst) and the very busy working lives of the teaching staff (who regularly have to teach for over 25 hours a week: an exhausting schedule even before we consider class preparation, assessment preparation, marking and moderation – not to mention open evenings, helping with recruitment and so forth). Hardly a place for introspection and scholarship.

And yet something must be going right. HE in FE provision has continued to expand over recent years, and students tend to describe their experiences on HE in FE programmes in positive ways. Indeed, some of the characteristics of HE in FE provision might be looked on with something akin to envy by lecturers in universities. The smaller class sizes and the opportunities for proper one-to-one tutorial support that the HE in FE environment provides are increasingly uncommon in 'mainstream' HE. Universities continue to establish new partnerships with FE colleges, who increasingly approach universities with ideas for new programmes and curricula, rather than the other way around. The quality of

HE in FE provision – which includes staffing as well as material resources – is regularly inspected (the inspection of HE in FE provision is discussed in Chapter 9) and is to a significant degree found to be of a good quality. HE in FE lecturers 'know their subject'.

So how does the FE sector itself understand the demands of research and scholarly activity? In 2012, the Association of Colleges (AoC – in effect, the professional body for FE colleges, founded in 1996) and the Learning and Skills Improvement Service (LSIS) published a document titled *HE in FE Guide*, which offers a definition of scholarship that is wider than the definitions usually found within universities. According to the *HE in FE Guide* (2012, page 50), scholarly activity includes:

- keeping up to date with the subject;
- curriculum development, particularly Foundation degrees, often with HEIs;
- curriculum development that involves research;
- updating ICT skills;
- taking higher qualifications – masters, doctorates and teaching qualifications;
- consultancy to industry and other agencies;
- industrial secondments or work shadowing;
- involvement with SSCs (Sector Skills Councils);
- research and publications;
- practitioner/applied research;
- personal development – action research and reading;
- attending staff development events within the college;
- attending conferences and workshops externally.

REFLECTIVE TASK

Take time to work through the AoC/LSIS scholarly activity list that appears above. To what extent are opportunities such as these made available within your college? Which of these – if any – are actively promoted as scholarly activities within HE in FE teams?

At first look, the different activities listed by AoC/LSIS all seem fine. But even allowing for the differences between research and scholarship that must exist between FE colleges and universities (which the document, quite rightly, acknowledges), some of the proposed areas of scholarly activity that are proposed here do seem to be problematic. Let us consider some of these activities in a little more detail. To begin with, it is difficult if not impossible to argue that attending conferences or workshops constitutes a form of scholarly activity. Similarly, if a teacher wishes to begin working with a sector skills council that is aligned to their subject specialism, such work might be seen as comparable with the kinds of work that university lecturers might undertake when engaging with their own subject specialist communities, such as organising a conference or reviewing journal articles prior to publication. And activities such as involvement in research and publications, or taking higher qualifications, are directly comparable to what might be expected of a lecturer in a university. So far it would seem that these definitions of scholarly activity would not seem out of place in a university – as opposed to a college – setting.

On the other hand, keeping up to date with the subject is specifically excluded from definitions of research and scholarly activity in HEIs. Attending staff development events within the college can hardly be understood as requiring scholarly work if the focus of the development event is procedural, administrative or focused very narrowly on quality or audit functions. Updating ICT skills is a necessary element of staying up to date, but can a training day focused on the use of interactive whiteboards in the classroom or setting up discussion threads on a virtual learning environment be seen as scholarly work? The danger here is that scholarship becomes overtaken – swallowed up, as it were – by a wider and more problematic definition of CPD. There is not much time for CPD in the timetable of the college lecturer, and what time is available tends to be used for formal CPD that is directed by college-wide policies or initiatives.

Scholarship is a potentially tricky topic of discussion, therefore. But what of research? Over a decade ago, impediments to research in FE colleges were summarised in terms of: lack of time and money; lack of a research culture; lack of value attached to research; and lack of opportunity for dissemination (Culham, 2001, page 27). How might these barriers be overcome?

THEORY FOCUS THEORY FOCUS **THEORY** FOCUS THEORY FOCUS

Modelling research activity in HE in FE

In a landmark article published in the *Journal of Vocational Education and Training* in 2003, three members of a larger research group exploring teaching and learning in FE – Graham Anderson and Sue Barton (both working at the time in a FE college) and Madeleine Wahlberg (a university-based lecturer) – proposed a number of different research models that might be applicable to the wider FE sector. While acknowledging that the prevailing conditions of the FE workplace makes the establishment of a research culture difficult (a situation that has not changed in the decade since this article was published), the authors of the article nonetheless highlight the benefits that being engaged in research bring to FE teachers. They argue that a combination of some of the models that they propose would be the optimal way through which to bring about a deep-rooted cultural shift in attitudes towards research and scholarship in FE colleges.

The article proposes eight different models of HE in FE. These, together with some critical and evaluative comments (which go beyond the themes discussed in the original article), are as follows:

1. FE staff study for higher degrees (masters degrees or doctorates)

Encouraging staff to study for higher degrees is an obvious step to take in seeking to establish a culture of research and scholarship. Masters level degrees frequently require students to engage in small-scale practitioner research, which can be of benefit to the institution. And university partners frequently require college-based staff to be qualified at postgraduate level if they are to teach a university programme. But such higher study can also be seen as a 'springboard' to a job at a university (it should be noted here that the three authors of this book all worked in FE colleges, teaching on HE in FE programmes, before moving to universities).

2. Appointing specialist research staff

Anderson et al. cite the work of LeGallais (2002) as being indicative of the kinds of excellent research that can be done by paid researchers working in colleges (it should be noted that LeGallais now works in a university). Other colleges have in the past also employed staff as researchers (Hillier and Thompson, 2005). However, the use of such specialists does not automatically equate to the encouragement of a more general research culture and has, since the article was published, declined.

3. The use of college data for research

As part of the day-to-day business of running a college, significant amounts of data are collected relating to attendance, progress and achievement and so forth. Anderson et al. note that the collection of such data is an aspect of the wider performativity cultures that characterise the sector more generally, and that the monitoring of such data is not, in itself, research (2003, page 509). However, it is worth pointing out that the use of existing data sets for *secondary research* is an increasingly well-established aspect of research work (Smith, 2008), and it is quite possible that such data could be useful in the context of appropriately framed research projects.

4. The provision of staff training and continuing professional development (CPD)

CPD, or the training and development of staff in a broader sense, must surely be seen as being an important element of establishing a culture of research and scholarship in HE in FE. But previous compulsory models of CPD in FE (the IfL's 30 hours target) cannot be seen as being sufficient in terms of building any serious capacity for HE in FE research. The managerialist agenda that controls CPD provision would seem to impose styles or types of further training for staff that are restricted to the business culture of colleges (Orr, 2008).

5. Opening up the FE sector to research by outside agencies

Over recent years, a number of different outside agencies have funded and conducted research in the learning and skills sector. Some of these are now defunct (such as the Learning and Skills Council) and others are in the process of becoming so (the Learning and Skills Improvement Service has lost its funding from the Department for Business, Innovation and Skills). Such initiatives are to be welcomed, not least as the FE sector remains relatively under-researched, but they tend to remain as research projects that are done 'to' rather than 'by' people in FE.

6. Adopting a university model for research

Asking colleges to 'behave' like universities – to bid for research grants, to focus on publication by research active staff and so forth – might seem 'logical', but it is doubtful that colleges could compete with universities for available resources for research (Anderson et al., 2003, page 510). Indeed, the increasing diversity of the university sector more generally, combined with current pressures on research funds and increasing competition between universities for research make such a move appear less and less desirable as well as less and less practicable.

7. Partnerships between HE and FE

Over the last decade there have been a number of examples of college and university partnerships that have made provision for research. Two recent large-scale research projects in the FE sector were planned and conducted as partnerships between university and college-based researchers and at one level can be seen as having built research capacity within the partner colleges rather than simply provided a route for the research-ers to move from colleges to universities (Ivaniç et al., 2009; James and Biesta, 2007). Some of the current research work being planned and conducted by the authors of this book also rests on a partnership model. However, this approach does rely on either suc-cessful funding (in order to be able to buy out FE staff) or significant amounts of good will and additional work (by FE staff – HE staff are expected to spend time engaged in research, as has been discussed, and have time for this in their workloads).

8. A research consortium

Anderson et al. propose a consortium model as a way of ensuring that the research agenda is owned by the FE colleges who wish to join (2003, page 510). While consortium arrange-ments have been used widely as a way of establishing and managing HE in FE provision more generally (usually, although not always, when HE programmes are run by a college on a franchise basis), the role of such consortia as drivers for research is less clear. Some consortia offer CPD and discounted routes to higher degrees for lecturers from 'partner' colleges, but others do not. Some consortia establish research groups and are successful in starting up research projects in which college as well as university staff work (Dixon et al., 2010). Others are not. As such, bearing in mind current restrictions on research funding, it seems unlikely that such provision will have the capacity to expand in the near future.

REFLECTIVE TASK

What might work best for you?

Although the ways in which Anderson et al. position research activities in HE in FE into eight catego-ries might seem to be somewhat artificial – it is more likely that more than one of these factors could be seen to be at work at any one particular time – they nonetheless provide a useful starting point for evaluating the potential for research at an individual level. Which of the processes that they describe might be available to you in the college where you work? Talk to colleagues who teach on other HE in FE programmes. Do different universities have different expectations of their partnership staff? For example, do they specify that partnership staff should hold Masters level degrees, or evidence other forms of scholarly activity?

Research and scholarship: critical responses, or making do?

It is not difficult to find articles in refereed academic journals that have been written by college lecturers. Similarly, many conferences that have a focus on the learning and skills sector offer opportunities for college-based researchers to present their findings from research work that is underway. And in recent years there has been something of a renaissance of the Learning and Skills Research Network (LSRN), after a period of inactivity. Some college lecturers, quite clearly, are engaging with research (as distinct from scholarship), and this can only be a benefit to the lecturers themselves, to their students (recent surveys indicate that students respond positively to lecturers who are seen as research active experts in their field), to their colleges (who can, quite rightly, refer to the research work of their lecturers when evaluating their HE provision) and to partner universities (who are, quite rightly, concerned to ensure that partnership staff are as far as possible appropriately qualified and as experienced as are the staff at the main university site).

Only a minority of college staff teaching HE in FE programmes are engaged in research, however. This is not a problem: as we have discussed, research is not part of 'the work' of the FE college and it is unrealistic, if not inappropriate, to expect research to be a significant feature of college life. Finding the time for research – or for doing a research degree – remains far from straightforward: time is a precious commodity, but many universities do still offer reductions in course fees to staff from partner colleges, which is to be commended. But if only a minority of staff are – or should be expected to be – engaging in research, surely it must be right to assume that all HE in FE staff are engaged in wider scholarly activity, if they are to move beyond 'reading to teach'? If we accept this to be the case, then it seems equally right that HE in FE staff – teachers and managers – need to continue to make the case for time for reading, for engaging in their subject that moves beyond merely what is needed in order to teach the curriculum, to encourage the wider, critical expertise that is characteristic of university teaching.

A SUMMARY OF KEY POINTS

During this chapter we have looked at the following key issues:
➢ Definitions of 'research' are common across HE and HE in FE; definitions of 'scholarly activity' are more contested, however.
➢ A number of cultural, organisational and practical barriers can be seen as impacting on research and scholarly activity in HE in FE.
➢ Different working relationships with partner universities can encourage research and scholarship, but there is no single 'best fit'.

Engaging in research and scholarship motivates and stimulates both staff and students, leading to an increased engagement in the teaching-learning process. Simply put, research and scholarship enhance HE teaching, and this in itself is sufficient reason for it to be encouraged by college HE in FE managers and asked for – demanded? – by HE in FE teaching staff (Feather, 2012b; Young, 2002). It is highly unlikely that current pressures of either time or resources in FE are going to be alleviated in the near future: as such, the encouragement of a wider scholarly culture will continue to rely on the temperament, motivation and 'above and beyond' professionalism of the individual lecturer, facilitated by those college managers who do see that while HE in FE is different from mainstream HE, it is also different from mainstream FE as well: it is a unique aspect of provision and requires consideration as such.

Branching options

Reflection

As you look back over this chapter, think about the ways in which engaging in research and scholarly activity might contribute to the 'HE ethos' (see also the discussion in Chapter 2) of your college. Talk with colleagues and compare your views. How might research or scholarly activity be encouraged in your own practice?

Analysis

It has been argued that research and scholarly activity are defined and practised in the FE sector in a manner that is rather different to the HE sector. What are the implications for parity between sectors of such an approach? *Why* should scholarly activity be defined in terms of institutional context as opposed to the needs of the HE curriculum?

Research

Although research of necessity involves significant intellectual effort, it is a process that also requires a lot of practical groundwork – and a good deal of patience. A useful first step is to explore the extent of any support that might be obtained from partner HE institutions: this might come in the form of fee support, for example, or access to research training programmes. Support structures such as these are not uncommon and are worth looking for.

REFERENCES REFERENCES REFERENCES REFERENCES REFERENCES

Anderson, G., Wahlberg, M. and Barton, S. (2003) Reflections and experiences of further education research in practice, *Journal of Vocational Education and Training,* 55(4): 499-516.

Association of Colleges/Learning and Skills Improvement Service (2012) *HE in FE Guide.* Available online at: www.aoc.co.uk/en/policy-and-advice/higher-education (accessed 03/06/13).

Avis, J. (2005) Beyond performativity: reflections on activist professionalism and the labour process in further education, *Journal of Education Policy,* 20(2): 209–22.

Culham, A. (2001) Practitioner-based research in FE: realities and problems, *College Research* Summer, 27–8.

Dixon, L., Jennings, A., Orr, K. and Tummons, J. (2010) Dominant discourses of pre-service teacher education and the exigencies of the workplace: an ethnographic study from English further education, *Journal of Vocational Education and Training,* 62(4): 381–93.

Feather, D. (2012a) Oh to be a scholar – an HE in FE perspective, *Journal of Further and Higher Education*, 36(2): 243–61.

Feather, D. (2012b) Do lecturers delivering higher education in further education desire to conduct research? *Research in Post-Compulsory Education,* 17(3): 335–47.

Gleeson, D., Davies, J. and Wheeler, E. (2005) On the making and taking of professionalism in the further education workplace, *British Journal of Sociology of Education,* 26(4): 445–60.

Hillier, Y. and Thompson, A. (eds) (2005) *Readings in Post-Compulsory Education*. London: Continuum.

Ivanič, R., Edwards, R., Barton, D., Martin-Jones, M., Fowler, Z., Hughes, B., Mannion, G., Miller, K., Satchwell, C. and Smith, J. (2009) *Improving Learning in College: Rethinking Literacies Across the Curriculum*. London: Routledge.

James, D. and Biesta, G. (2007) *Improving Learning Cultures in Further Education*. London: Routledge.

LeGallais, T. (2002) Research: a valuable tool in the process of change and innovation? *Learning and Skills Journal,* 5(2): 51–2.

Orr, K. (2008) Room for improvement? The impact of compulsory professional development for teachers in England's further education sector, *Journal of In-Service Education,* 34(1): 97–108.

Orr, K. and Simmons, R. (2010) Dual identities: the in-service teacher trainee experience in the English further education sector, *Journal of Vocational Education and Training,* 62(1): 75–88.

Parry, G. and Thompson, A. (2002) *Closer By Degrees: The Past, Present and Future of Higher Education in Further Education Colleges*. London: Learning and Skills Development Agency.

Shain, F. and Gleeson, D. (1999) Under new management: changing conceptions of teacher professionalism and policy in the further education sector, *Journal of Education Policy,* 14(4): 445–62.

Smith, E. (2008) *Using Secondary Data in Educational and Social Research*. Maidenhead: Open University Press.

Spenceley, L. (2006) Smoke and mirrors: an examination of the concept of professionalism within the FE sector, *Research in Post-Compulsory Education,* 11(3): 289–302.

Tummons, J. and Duckworth, V. (2012) *Doing Your Research Project in the Lifelong Learning Sector*. Maidenhead: McGraw Hill.

Wilson, A. and Wilson, B. (2011) Pedagogy of the repressed: research and professionality within HE in FE, *Research in Post-Compulsory Education,* 16(4): 465–78.

Young, P. (2002) Scholarship is the word that dare not speak its name. Lecturers' experiences of teaching on a higher education programme in a further education college, *Journal of Further and Higher Education,* 26(3): 273–86.

8

Managing HE in FE

By the end of this chapter you will be able to:

- identify key debates surrounding middle management roles and responsibilities in the FE sector;
- relate these debates to HE in FE provision;
- identify ways in which the management of HE in FE provision can be made more effective.

Introduction: course and programme management in the further education sector

Although new members of staff in a FE college might expect to be able to focus on their teaching, learning and assessment practice, it is not uncommon for them to be given additional responsibilities for course or programme administration, even at a relatively early stage of their careers. A college lecturer might, for example, have to establish a working relationship with an external verifier, attend standardisation meetings hosted by an awarding body such as City and Guilds or NCFE and acquaint themselves with all of those procedures – admissions, recording achievement data and so forth – that are required for the course to run successfully. And this applies equally to those members of staff who deliver HE in FE provision as well. A lecturer who is asked to teach on one or more of the HE in FE programmes that a college might be offering may have to attend an induction day at a partner university, get to know the university's admissions policy and procedure, attend moderation events and examination boards and so forth. There is a lot of administration and paperwork (e-mails, websites and virtual learning environments notwithstanding) involved in being a lecturer. There are forms to fill in, handbooks to read, systems and procedures to learn, new e-mail contacts to add to Outlook and so on. And as well as all of this, lecturers have to do some actual teaching.

At the other end of the scale – or, more accurately, at the top as opposed to the bottom of the organisational chart – the college senior management team (SMT) enact policy and decide on the strategic direction of the college. They respond to regional and national policy, meet with employers and funding agencies, and report to the college board of governors. And for any college that delivers HE programmes there will usually be one member of the senior management team with overall responsibility for leading the HE provision – an assistant principal for HE (or similar – job titles vary somewhat across the sector). And finally, positioned between senior managers and lecturers are middle managers. Middle management is the term used to refer to those members of staff who maintain a (somewhat reduced) lecturing role alongside the management of a particular area of college provision – usually (although not always) at curriculum or programme level, with responsibilities for course-specific budgets, staffing, recruitment, and so forth.

In this chapter, we shall focus on this more routine, 'day-to-day' management of HE in FE provision. The focus here is not on the kinds of strategic leadership that HE in FE provision requires within colleges and which is practised by assistant principals (although we suggest that senior managers would still benefit from a continued consideration of the issues discussed in this chapter). Instead, we concentrate on the routine operations that such programmes require, the ways in which these operations are aligned to course or curriculum management within the mainstream FE curriculum, and the ways in which HE in FE management stands apart from the main body of college provision and what this implies for college middle management.

REFLECTIVE TASK

Before reading on, take the time to think about the way in which module or course management is organised within the college that you work in – and, if appropriate, within other colleges that you have worked in or have visited. Is the management of HE in FE provision done differently in these colleges, or do such roles appear to be the same, irrespective of the level of the course in question? Do you think that managing a programme at NQF level 3 is the same, or different, or 'harder', than managing a foundation degree at levels 4 and 5? What kinds of issues are common across programmes at different levels? And what issues might be unique to HE-level provision?

Middle managers in further education

In a way, it might be easier to begin to define middle managers in colleges by saying who they are not. They are not members of the senior management team, and they do not necessarily hold qualifications in management (nor, for that matter, do many members of senior management teams). They do not manage only those areas of the curriculum that they have previously taught. But they are not 'only' lecturers. They are not defined or positioned primarily in terms of their teaching. They do not usually influence of inform the work of senior management; nor do they always enjoy harmonious relations with the lecturers whom they manage. They are, in many ways, 'stuck' in the middle – but they are not unimportant to the success of the college as a whole.

So who are college middle managers? We shall explore the position of middle managers in FE colleges in more detail (and from a research perspective) later in the chapter, but for now we shall provide a brief outline of what they do. They are the 'curriculum leaders', 'programme leaders' or 'section leaders' who are responsible for the routine management of areas of the curriculum during the academic cycle, from recruitment to certification. They agree expenses claims and carry out annual appraisals. They sign off requests for attending continuing professional development (CPD) events, and (from time to time) agree to employ hourly paid tutors if workloads become unmanageable. They monitor recruitment, retention and achievement so that college financial targets are met, and collate end-of-year reports for awarding bodies (including universities). Middle managers do not make policy, as such, but they are responsible for enacting it – including at a classroom level: the vast majority of middle managers continue to have a substantial teaching role within their curriculum area. Middle managers occupy a sometimes-awkward position, therefore. In part, this is due to their position on the organisational chart, sandwiched between lecturers and principals, acting on the one hand as the conduits for college strategy and on the other as a buffer between senior managers and lecturers. And in part this is due to their role as part-lecturer and part-manager, teaching and assessing alongside colleagues whom they evaluate, observe and manage. In this way, middle managers straddle two very different approaches or mind-sets to the work of the FE college, and it is to these two mind-sets that we shall now turn.

Middle managers, professionalism and managerialism

Rightly or wrongly, relations between lecturing staff and managers – in the FE sector – have been characterised as cautious at best and hostile at worst. Current debates tend to revolve around two key factors. First, there is the impact of the incorporation of FE colleges 20 years ago, which was accompanied by significant changes to the working conditions of lecturers (for example, changes to existing contracts, the growth of 'zero-hours' contracts and of the use of part-time casual staff, changed pay structures that saw the pay gap between school teachers and college lecturers get larger, and increases in teaching workloads) during a period when the remuneration of senior managers increased considerably. Second, running alongside these changes, there is the emergence and growth of managerial cultures in FE. Managerialism is here understood as being a belief that professionals (lecturers) need to be managed in order that the service (education) that they provide is of the best 'quality', drawing on private sector methods (because the 'liberal' public sector is too inefficient and wasteful). This managerial ethos exists in contrast to what has been termed the 'professional' ethos that is seen as embodying the perspectives of lecturers (Randle and Brady, 1997).

Thus, professionalism rests on:

* the learning experience of students and the value of the teacher;
* the use of resources according to educational need;
* teachers' autonomy, and trust on the part of managers.

Whereas managerialism rests on:

* student enrolment and completion, and income generation;
* resources used according to 'value for money';
* surveillance of teachers' work through targets, performance indicators, evaluations and the like.

This is something of an over-simplification, not least as definitions of professionalism can vary considerably and have implications for the broader ways in which we can understand the work that lecturers – and colleges – can or ought to do (Hayes et al., 2007; Robson, 2000; Tummons, 2010). And such an over-simplification runs the risk of prolonging a debate about the nature of teaching and of management in FE which requires more careful and reflective consideration (Lumby and Tomlinson, 2000). But the key debate is clear: should the ethos that shapes the work of FE lecturers – and, by extension, of HE in FE lecturers as well – be an ethos of autonomous professionalism, or of managerialism? Is there any space for compromise or collaboration between these, or will the 'professionalism' of the lecturer always come into conflict with the demands of managers? And how will the middle manager, sitting between lecturers and senior managers and practising both kinds of work, respond?

RESEARCH FOCUS RESEARCH FOCUS **RESEARCH** FOCUS RESEARCH FOCUS

Exploring responses to managerialism in further education

In 1999, Farzana Shain and Denis Gleeson published research that explored the ways in which FE teachers were responding to changes in their working environments as a result of the incorporation of college six years earlier, and the subsequent emergence of managerialism in the FE workplace. They argued that meanings of 'professionalism' were changing in response to wider changes across the sector. They identified three ways in which lecturers responded to the demands of managerialism (Shain and Gleeson, 1999, pages 453–9):

1. Rejection and resistance. 'Older' members of staff resisted the marketisation of FE, rejecting the notion that colleges should be seen as competing for students and 'selling' education and training as a product. Instead, they maintained a commitment to an 'old' public sector ethos that defined professionalism in terms of autonomy and pedagogy.
2. Compliance. Some 'newer' members of staff positioned themselves in opposition to those who rejected and resisted, arguing that 'older' staff were complacent and 'stuck in the past'. These staff acknowledged the need for job security and of acceptance of the 'new realism' of managerialism.
3. Strategic compliance. The majority of staff in colleges fell between these two camps. They acknowledged both 'new' managerial approaches as well as 'old' models of professionalism. They were willing to work within the new FE culture and to improvise or exploit it where necessary if they believed that such actions would benefit their students.

Shain and Gleeson's research (which over time has proved to be influential) highlighted quite clearly the different ways in which members of staff in FE colleges defined themselves as professional. Does being a professional mean trusting the autonomous judgement of the lecturer, or adhering to the quality assurance requirements of the management team? Should definitions of 'professionalism' (if we actually need them at all) be established by lecturers, by managers or by policy makers?

There is insufficient space here to explore the growth of different models of 'professionalism' in FE (or in any other place): the important point to note here is that different people have very different ideas about what colleges should do and how they should go about doing it. And it is the college middle manager who often has to balance these very different, and difficult, perspectives (Briggs, 2001).

Exploring the work of middle managers in the further education sector

How can the position of middle managers in FE be accurately defined? Here, we follow the work of Briggs (2002), and equate the 'middle manager' role with being the head of a curriculum area or subject department, answering to a head of faculty, and managing a teaching team. Such a curriculum area may be quite broad, and different subject areas will be grouped together for different reasons. In some colleges, there may be an attempt to collect subject areas together that all form part of a larger, recognisable curriculum area. In other colleges, subject areas may be grouped together for management and administrative purposes purely for reasons of size or convenience, or because one or more programmes don't really 'fit' anywhere else. Consequently, the curriculum head may be more-or-less experienced in the teaching of some of the subject areas that they are responsible for. This can cause problems when establishing working relations with lecturers, who may feel that 'their' subject area – what resources are needed, how it should be taught, what the needs of the students are – is not properly understood or appreciated by their curriculum leader. At the same time, the fact that curriculum heads continue to carry substantial teaching workloads leads to their being identified as 'one of us' by lecturers who might see them as being 'go-betweens' between the lecturing staff and the senior management team. In fact, the reality of college life is that middle managers tend to have relatively little influence on policy or governance – but, at the same time, they are a vital element in the enactment of these same policies. So what is it, exactly, that they do?

Allowing for institutional variations, the role of middle managers in FE tends to revolve around the following four key issues (Marsden and Youde, 2010):

1. Annual course/curriculum area evaluation

This report usually forms part of the wider college quality assurance process (as discussed in the following chapter) and will go into the college self-assessment report (SAR), which in turn forms part of the Ofsted inspection process.

2. Curriculum planning and management

This will include oversight of schemes of work and assessment schedules, resource planning and purchasing, and timetabling. It may also require liaison with awarding bodies, employers and other stakeholders.

3. Management of the course team

This will include the allocation of teaching to individual members of staff (made more complex when managing a mixture of full-time, part-time and hourly-paid staff), observations of teaching for the purposes of quality monitoring, and annual staff appraisals.

4. Attendance, progression and achievement

This will include not only collating information from individual members of the teaching team, but also presenting and evaluating this information at meetings of the college senior management team (SMT).

Middle managers in HE in FE: bridging the two sectors

The ways in which the management and organisation of HE in FE is implemented varies across the FE sector. In larger colleges with substantial HE provision, dedicated HE facilities might be found alongside a specific HE management team and lecturers who spend the majority – perhaps even all – of their time working on HE programmes. In colleges where HE provision is on a smaller scale, lecturers and managers will usually be found working across both HE and FE programmes (Parry et al., 2012). As such, managers of

HE provision will often encounter issues and problems that are familiar across the sector as a whole (as discussed above), as well as others that are unique to HE.

Sector-wide issues for HE in FE managers

How might the four key issues for FE middle managers impact on the work of HE in FE managers? We shall evaluate each of these in turn.

Annual course/curriculum area evaluation

Universities are by no means immune to the pressures of managerialism and audit culture, although these are arguably less of a burden in HE than in FE. But the requirements of quality assurance departments are similar across both sectors, and these will need to be considered by HE in FE managers. In some cases, this simply means substituting one end-of-year evaluation template with another. In other cases, it can mean having to complete two annual reports – one for the college and one for the partner university. In turn, these reports might also inform other quality assurance processes. These might in turn relate to university-led processes (quality monitoring visits to partner FE colleges, for example, are a common feature of HE in FE quality assurance) or to external processes such as audit by the Quality Assurance Agency for Higher Education (Parry et al., 2012).

Curriculum planning and management

The extent to which a partner university might inform curriculum planning can vary. For programmes that have been written by college teams and then validated by a HE partner, a considerable degree of autonomy might be found. For programmes which are franchised from the HE partner, on the other hand, it may be necessary for modules to be delivered and then assessed according to a central timetable. This might be due to the need to align the programme with university-based systems and timetables (such as the timing of assessment boards, for example). Or this might be due to the need to ensure a standardised delivery model for a franchised programme that is delivered simultaneously at several partner colleges. Similarly, course documentation (handbooks, module guides, assessment templates and so forth) might be generated at the college, or supplied by the university.

Management of the course team

Most HE in FE lecturers continue to teach on FE programmes. As such, the issues that HE in FE team managers have to face are very similar to those faced by other middle managers in FE colleges. Some of these might be described as 'routine': recruitment, managing holidays, carrying out annual evaluations, or organising cover when a colleague is poorly. Others, however, are arguably more acute when considered within a HE in FE context. Disagreements concerning the qualifications needed by staff to teach HE provide a good example: recent research has indicated that, notwithstanding the well-established maxim that you should be qualified at 'one level above' the course that you teach, one job description for HE in FE asked for applicants with qualifications at level 3 only, with a commitment to achieve level 4 in the future, for a HE childcare leader responsible for managing a foundation degree (Creasy, 2013). The value of scholarly activity is another: according to research by Harwood and Harwood (2004), some senior managers do not think that scholarly activity is needed when 'only' teaching level 4. These issues provide good examples of the ways in which middle managers face conflicting pressures from senior managers on the one had, and their teaching team on the other (Shain and Gleeson, 1999).

Attendance, progression and achievement

The need to maintain student numbers and to maximise student achievement is characteristic of the entire FE sector, and this pressure has become more acute in recent years, not least as a consequence of the imposition of managerialism. Ensuring that HE in FE programmes remain viable is particularly complex, not least as the sizes of student cohorts is normally quite small. Consequently, it is important for middle managers to work to ensure that barriers to participation and engagement are identified, and that steps are taken to minimise their impact. This issue is not unique to HE in FE, but research indicates that the kinds of barriers that are experienced by HE in FE students are qualitatively different to those experienced by mainstream FE students (Burton et al., 2011). In the same way, the provision of specific interventions such as tailored study skills programmes has been shown to help retain viable group sizes in HE in FE (an issue that we shall return to below).

REFLECTIVE TASK

REFLECTIVE TASK

Managing HE in FE provision can be seen as involving the same kinds of problems – and responses – as might emerge during the management of any other curriculum area within a typical FE college. To what extent do your experiences, or the experiences of colleagues, illustrate the kinds of themes discussed in the research articles referred to here? How might a consideration of the research literature that relates to the management of HE in FE provision have a practical impact on how HE in FE might be run in your college?

It might not always seem that way to people who read them, but research articles are often intended to have something to say that is of practical – and not 'just' academic or theoretical – consequence. It is perhaps to be regretted that staff in FE colleges do not have as much time to read journals as they might like. Access to journals should not be a problem, however: for HE in FE staff, some level of membership of the library at the franchising university will include access to academic journals which are almost all available online. As such, managers as well as lecturers should be encouraged to use whatever time they have for scholarly activity (as discussed in the preceding chapter) to read research that will have a practical impact. In our experience, senior managers in colleges are usually (although by no means always) more interested in 'what works', rather than in 'what is of academic interest'. The right research paper can, therefore, be a useful spur to action.

RESEARCH FOCUS   RESEARCH   FOCUS   **RESEARCH** FOCUS   RESEARCH   FOCUS

Predictors of retention and achievement in HE in FE

In a research article published in 2010, Cathy Schofield and Harriet Dismore provided an account of research that looked at data from over 400 students who were enrolled on both foundation degrees and higher national diplomas at a large FE college offering over 25 such programmes in different curriculum areas. They found that when trying to predict students' progress – in terms of the grades

(Continued)

(Continued)

they would receive across their first year of study, against numbers of student withdrawals – that two factors emerged as being significant. The first was the level – not the type – of the students' prior qualifications: the higher the prior qualification, the higher the average grade. The second was the age of the students: older students were more likely to complete their studies than younger students. The key practical suggestion made in the article was for the provision of tailored study skills support to new HE in FE students in place of existing generic provision, in order to account for these significant factors.

For the HE in FE curriculum manager who is concerned as to the viability of their student cohorts, such research is of immediate practical benefit. Maintaining a minimum group size is a financial matter: courses become uneconomical if group sizes are too small because the income generated will be so much smaller than the cost of running the programme. But it is an academic matter as well. Certainly, full-time undergraduates in universities sometimes complain that class sizes are too large (visions of packed lecture halls spring to mind, although this is not in itself a problem). But the class sizes offered by FE colleges (indeed, much HE in FE provision actively advertises small group sizes as a benefit to college-based study) should not be allowed to become too small.

Similarly, other issues that – we suggest – might be of relevance to managers of HE in FE provision in colleges and which could be explored and resolved in part through recourse to research literature include:

- the importance of establishing good working relationships with partner universities, so that opportunities for staff development can be exploited, resources can be shared and matters around teaching and research can be discussed in a collegial manner (Harwood and Harwood, 2004);
- the negative impacts of FE governance and provision on HE in FE courses, so that – where necessary – the attitude of the college can be made more amenable to the aspirations of the HE ethos in such practical matters as time for preparation and scholarly activity, recognition of the link between scholarship and teaching, library stock and opening hours, the provision of appropriate teaching accommodation and so forth (Young, 2002).

A SUMMARY OF **KEY POINTS**

During this chapter we have looked at the following key issues:
- The position of middle managers in FE within a managerialist culture following the incorporation of colleges 20 years ago.
- The ways in which HE provision within FE colleges generates particular tensions and issues for managers.
- The use of research literature to explore and inform possible solutions for these tensions and issues.

Middle managers in FE colleges occupy an ambiguous space, positioned partly among senior managers and partly among college lecturers, but without properly belonging to either group.

Arguably, the management of HE provision within a college provides a further level of complexity to the position held by these managers. The culture of HE – even allowing for the growth of the audit culture in universities – is markedly different from that of FE. This is not to say that colleges should try to replicate what happens in universities, because they cannot. And in fact universities are more complex and less homogeneous than some people might think. The HE sector is diverse, and college-based provision is, at one level, simply another aspect of that diversity. For managers of HE in FE curricula, therefore, being able to cope with and then to manage this diversity is, arguably, a necessary function, irrespective of the size or nature of the HE programme in question. Which, in a way, is not so different from any other middle management role within the FE sector. But there is one key difference, as discussed in Chapter 2: the HE ethos.

Branching options

Reflection

To what extent have you received any formal professional development or training when taking on a managerial or course/programme area leadership role? Often, such training might involve induction into those college systems and processes that the programme needs to use in order to respond to the direction set by senior managers. But how often does it offer the time and space to reflect on how to reconcile the different discourses of FE – with its emphasis on audit, managerial control and the bottom line – with HE – with its emphasis on scholarship, autonomy and trust? Can these values be encouraged through the actions of middle managers?

Analysis

The complex organisational cultures of the FE sector are quite different from those of the HE sector (although universities do differ considerably in terms of how they are structured and managed). In FE, researchers talk about 'balkanisation' (Lea et al., 2003). In HE, researchers talk about 'tribes' (Becher and Trowler, 2001). How might college-based HE provision be made sense of in these terms? Should it be seen as a thing apart from the mainstream work or business of an FE college, or should it be seen as providing a natural progression route for students who can elect to study from level 3 through to level 5 (and perhaps higher) at their local college? And to what extent are such progression routes desirable, as opposed to merely pragmatic?

Research

HE in FE is relatively under-researched, although during the last few years a stream of worthwhile and engaging articles has been published (many of which are referenced throughout this book). Management aspects of HE in FE are similarly under-researched, although educational management itself is a well-established field of scholarly activity. It remains the case that although teachers in the post-compulsory sector have to be quali-fied to teach (notwithstanding the changes to the curriculum that are being published as this book is being written), managers do not have to be qualified to manage. As such, the ways in which managers learn how to be managers deserve critical investigation.

REFERENCES REFERENCES REFERENCES REFERENCES REFERENCES

Becher, T. and Trowler, P. (2001) *Academic Tribes and Territories* (2nd edition). Maidenhead: Open University Press/SRHE.

Briggs, A. (2001) Academic middle managers in further education: reflections on leadership, *Research in Post-Compulsory Education,* 6(2): 223–36.

Briggs, A. (2002) Facilitating the role of middle managers in further education, *Research in Post-Compulsory Education,* 7(1): 63–78.

Burton, K., Lloyd, M. and Griffiths, C. (2011) Barriers to learning for mature students studying HE in an FE college, *Journal of Further and Higher Education,* 35(1): 25–36.

Creasy, R. (2013) HE Lite: exploring the problematic position of HE in FECs, *Journal of Further and Higher Education,* 37(1): 38–53.

Harwood, J. and Harwood, D. (2004) Higher education in further education: delivering higher education in a further education context – a study of five South West colleges, *Journal of Further and Higher Education,* 28(2).

Hayes, D., Marshall, T. and Turner, A. (eds) (2007) *A Lecturer's Guide to Further Education*. Maidenhead: McGraw Hill.

Lea, J., Hayes, D., Armitage, A., Lomas, L. and Markless, S. (eds) (2003) *Working in Post-Compulsory Education*. Maidenhead: Open University Press.

Lumby, J. and Tomlinson, H. (2000) Principals speaking: managerialism and leadership in further education, *Research in Post-Compulsory Education,* 5(2): 139–51.

Marsden, F. and Youde, A. (2010) Administration and Course Management, in J. Avis, R. Fisher and R. Thompson (eds) *Teaching in Lifelong Learning: A Guide to Theory and Practice.* Maidenhead: McGraw Hill.

Parry, G., Callender, C., Scott, P. and Temple, P. (2012) *Understanding Higher Education in Further Education Colleges*. London: Department for Business, Innovation and Skills.

Randle, K. and Brady, N. (1997) Managerialism and professionalism in the 'Cinderella service', *Journal of Vocational Education and Training*, 49(1): 121–39.

Robson, J. (2000) A Profession in Crisis: Status, culture and identity in the further education college, in L. Hall and K. Marsh (eds) *Professionalism, Policies and Values*. London: Greenwich University Press.

Schofield, C. and Dismore, H. (2010) Predictors of retention and achievement of higher education students within a further education context, *Journal of Further and Higher Education,* 34(2): 207–21.

Shain, F. and Gleeson, D. (1999) Under new management: changing conceptions of teacher professionalism and policy in the further education sector, *Journal of Education Policy,* 14(4): 445–62.

Tummons, J. (2010) *Becoming a Professional Tutor in the Lifelong Learning Sector* (2nd edition). Exeter: Learning Matters.

Young, P. (2002) Scholarship is the word that dare not speak its name: lecturers' experiences of teaching on an HE programme in an FE college, *Journal of Further and Higher Education,* 26(3): 273–86.

9

Quality assurance in college-based higher education

By the end of this chapter you will be able to:

- identify the relevant quality assurance (QA) procedures for your HE courses;
- discuss issues relating to responsibility for the course, students and their *experience* within collaborative provision;
- discuss the impact of the National Student Survey;
- recognise the role of external examination;
- prepare appropriate documentation for QA purposes (validation).

Introducing quality assurance in college-based higher education

Anyone working in FE will be all too familiar with inspections, audits and the whole gamut of quality assurance procedures. Student satisfaction questionnaires (or happy sheets as some refer to them), Ofsted, observations of teaching and learning, self-assessment forms are all features of FE courses at every level. Until recently, however, HE was relatively free of much of this paperwork and even HE provision in FE was based around the notion of professional trust rather than audit criteria. That has been transformed, even for universities' own courses that are delivered on their own campuses. The wind of audit has blown into HE and FE tutors will recognise many of the QA processes that are now expected there. Certainly, the quality procedures in most colleges will be thorough and adaptive enough to respond to what is required for any higher-level courses. We should always remember, too, that all of these procedures, processes and systems are designed to ensure our students have a useful, positive experience, which can easily be forgotten within all the bureaucracy of quality assurance. Nevertheless, there are differences between regulations and procedures in FE and HE, which can lead to tensions, especially if the HE provision in a college is very small or when it is unclear who has specific responsibility for quality assurance for HE courses. In this chapter we will look at some of the features of QA integral to HE in FE and in particular we will discuss what is expected of tutors. We will concentrate on the systems and procedures that are specific to HE provision funded directly or indirectly by HEFCE since this is different to the usual FE regime for quality assurance under Ofsted. Let us start, however, by making some more general observations that will help us to pose the right questions about QA and our own responsibilities.

Traditionally, the most significant difference between colleges and universities has been that colleges run courses that lead to qualifications awarded by external bodies such as City and Guilds, or indeed a local university. Universities, on the other hand, award their own qualifications. For QA this has meant, very broadly, that universities are checked against their own criteria and procedures whereas FE colleges are checked against externally created criteria and procedures. With recent political moves to give colleges the power to award their own degrees (currently a very small minority and only at foundation degree level) this distinction may become blurred, but for the moment it remains quite useful. It means that tutors involved on HE courses need to locate the appropriate quality procedures, rather than produce their own, and then they have to identify what they need to do to fulfil those criteria. That sounds easy, but there are two factors that complicate matters. First of all, there are two organisations involved, the FE college and the university or awarding body such as CILEX (the Chartered Institute of Legal Executives). So, which one is answerable if something goes wrong? Which organisation is ultimately responsible for the students, the FE college or the university?

The second complicating factor is that procedures are frequently altered. As we have seen throughout this book HE in FE provision is constantly changing and nowhere more so than in relation to the quality assurance of courses. HE in FE has found itself at the centre of both political arguments over the stated need to improve the skills of the nation's workforce and political arguments over social justice through widening participation in education. As a result of this political importance and the simultaneous lack of political consensus we can expect more adjustments to national procedures. For example, from 2013 the Integrated Quality and Enhancement Review (IQER), which was designed specifically to consider HE in FE colleges in England, is to be replaced by a new review method called the Review of College Higher Education, which we will consider below. The old IQER system had only been in place for six years, and it had replaced the older Academic Review of subjects.

The kind of major change involved in the new Review is at a national, often statutory level, but there are also frequent modifications in QA criteria and procedures at an institutional level. Forms may change; expectations of feedback for students may become standardised; rules for giving students an extension to deadline may tighten. The tutor needs to keep abreast of these changes. In order to do that we shall first consider which bodies are in charge of HE in FE courses.

PRACTICAL TASK PRACTICAL TASK **PRACTICAL TASK** PRACTICAL TASK **PRACTICAL TASK**

Course teams should have a clear process to keep themselves informed of any changes in QA processes and requirements. Where do you need to look to find out about the current criteria and procedures for your programme? How will you know if these alter?

Which body controls regulations and quality on a course?

The answer to that question is not entirely straightforward. We have seen previously in this book that college-based HE is funded in three main ways: directly by HEFCE; indirectly by HEFCE through franchising arrangements; and finally by other non-HEFCE sources, such as the Skills Funding Agency. Depending on their source of funding, HE in

FE courses are scrutinised by two separate quality assurance bodies. Directly and indirectly funded undergraduate education (prescribed higher education) comes under the Quality Assurance Agency for Higher Education (QAA); provision funded by the SFA (non-prescribed higher education) comes under Ofsted. Teacher education courses funded through HEFCE are, however, also subject to Ofsted's quality regime. This means that two courses at the same academic level leading to similar awards can be inspected by different organisations. This division is also mirrored in the way that data are collected. Data for HE students who are registered at HEIs and taught in FE colleges are collected by the Higher Education Statistics Agency (HESA). Data on HE students registered at colleges but not attached to HEIs are collected by the Data Agency. So, to check what quality procedures apply to your course, you need to check how it is funded. The majority will come under the auspices of the QAA.

The role of the Quality Assurance Agency: benchmarks and subject specifications

The QAA is the preeminent body for the assurance of quality in HE in the UK and almost everything we discuss in this chapter comes under its remit. The QAA has been around since 1997 and its primary role is *to review and report on the performance of providers of higher education with regard to standards of awards and the quality of provision*. It is arguably more collaborative in its approach than Ofsted is in colleges since the QAA works *with higher education institutions to define academic standards and quality*. This reflects the culture of peer review, which still pervades so many aspects of HE work from journals to external examiners' reports. The QAA is responsible for the *UK Quality Code for Higher Education* (more usually known simply as the *Quality Code*), which sets out what is required of all UK HE providers to ensure that students are given a high-quality educational experience. The Quality Code was introduced in 2012 and it provides a shared basis for HE providers to set, describe and assure their own academic standards. To return to that difference with FE colleges, HE providers use the code to design their own policies for maintaining their institutions' academic standards and quality.

The definitions used within the code are useful when discussing QA more generally:

- *Academic standards* are the minimum level of achievement that you have to reach to succeed on a course and achieve the qualification. These threshold standards should not vary from one higher education provider to another.
- *Academic quality* is how well a higher education provider supports students in their learning: the teaching, the support available, the assessment, and the resources available.
- *Quality assurance* is the process for checking that the standards and quality of higher education provision meet agreed expectations.

The QAA also produces subject benchmark statements that set out requirements for degrees in a wide range of subject areas. These statements describe what is essential within a subject or discipline and they define *what can be expected of a graduate in terms of the abilities and skills needed to develop understanding or competence in the subject*. These statements should not be considered like a national curriculum for HE, or even like a BTEC award specification. They are flexible and they are intended to assist in the design of programmes within a given academic field. Here is an extract from the benchmark statements relating to education studies which illustrates the scope and tone of these statements:

> *A necessary feature of a bachelor's degree with honours in education studies is an intellectually rigorous study of educational processes, and the cultural, political and historical contexts within which they are embedded. While individual courses within degree programmes may have a focus upon particular age groups, or learning and teaching, or particular contexts and education systems, they will provide students with opportunities to engage in critical reflection and debate. Students should have the opportunity to engage with a number of different perspectives and to evaluate aims and values, means and ends, and the validity of the education issues in question.*

Being familiar with the Quality Code and relevant subject benchmarks is necessary for HE tutors and managers in colleges when validating a new course leading to an HE award. You should refer to the code and how meeting its criteria have shaped your new course validation submission. We will return to validation processes at the end of this chapter.

The QAA also inspects organisations providing HE awards through an Institutional Review and their criteria and reports are available on the QAA website. Once again this process is relatively new, only starting in 2011, and awarding organisations can normally expect a review every six years or so.

Finally, the QAA is responsible for the inspection of collaborative provision; that is when colleges run courses leading to university awards. The QAA ensures that a degree course in fashion taken at a college in Stockport or Yeovil has the same rigour and standards as the same degree course taken at the awarding university, or indeed at any other UK institution. Many tutors and managers involved with HE in colleges will first encounter the QAA in this role of inspecting a university's provision run through colleges or other providers. We focus on this process, the Review of College Higher Education, in the next section.

Review of College Higher Education

As we have seen, in September 2013 the Review of College Higher Education (RCHE) replaced the Integrated Quality and Enhancement Review (IQER) method that ran from 2007. The RCHE is the new means of reviewing HE provided by FE colleges in England. The RCHE is based on the Institutional Review of higher education institutions described in the previous section, but it has been adapted for FE colleges. The following extract from the QAA website identifies the purpose of the RCHE.

> *The core aim of RCHE is to examine whether colleges provide qualifications of an appropriate academic standard and a student experience of an acceptable quality. The review team makes judgements on how the college:*
>
> *1. sets and maintains threshold academic standards*
>
> *2. manages the quality of students' learning opportunities*
>
> *3. enhances its educational provision*

4. manages the quality of its information.

The new method is designed to be flexible and adaptable to change. The method may need to change in response to future policy and legislative developments, including the introduction of a less burdensome, more risk-based approach to quality assurance.

(www.qaa.ac.uk/InstitutionReports/types-of review/RCHE/Pages/default.aspx)

The new RCHE process comprises both a core element, which is applied to all colleges, and one or more specific thematic elements, which will change annually. The common core element will examine the effectiveness of the policies, structures and processes that a college uses to maintain academic standards, quality, information and enhancement. The thematic element in the review has a rather different purpose. It is intended to allow flexibility within the review process to consider issues of 'legitimate public interest or concern' and to explore a college's engagement with these issues in relation to quality assurance. These themes will react to changing circumstances and this new thematic element is designed to promote development through the sharing of good practice across HE providers. It is worth remembering, though, that in order to achieve consistency and comparability of review findings the thematic element will not be subject to a judgement. Instead, the review report will provide a descriptive commentary on the thematic element. The two themes to be considered in the first reviews are the First-Year Student Experience and Student Involvement in Quality Assurance and Enhancement.

The QAA website has much more information and a link to a handbook for colleges which will help you prepare for these reviews.

As this crucial RCHE is new we cannot comment on any of its findings or reports, but we can learn something from the former IQER and what it tells us about collaborative provision between colleges and HE institutions. A government report published in June 2012 entitled Understanding Higher Education in Further Education stated:

Between 2008–09 and 2010–11, 165 summative reviews were completed. The reviewers had 'confidence' in the standards of provision in all but three cases, two of which resulted in 'limited confidence' and one of 'no confidence'. Assessments were also made on the quality of learning opportunities. These resulted in 'confidence' judgements in all but two instances: one of 'limited confidence' and the other of 'no confidence'

(Parry et al., 2012, page 56)

In other words, the QAA has had confidence in HE provided in FE colleges in the overwhelming number of cases that it has looked at.

PRACTICAL TASK PRACTICAL TASK **PRACTICAL TASK** PRACTICAL TASK **PRACTICAL TASK**

Go on to the QAA website (www.qaa.ac.uk/INSTITUTIONREPORTS/Pages/default.aspx) and find reports for your institution or for the HEI with which you work. What are the strengths and weaknesses? How do these reflect in your own courses? How would you address the weaknesses?

National Student Survey

The National Student Survey (NSS) has become more and more significant since its inception in 2005 (HE in FE students have only been involved since 2008). Many universities and colleges use the survey's results in their promotional materials and the results are also available to prospective students to help them in choosing their institution. The NSS is carried out for HEFCE and it asks undergraduates in their final year to provide anonymous feedback on how satisfied they have been with their courses. Students on flexible courses, such as many HE in FE courses, will be asked to participate as they near the end of their course but not necessarily in their final year. The survey results are then published in a nationally recognised format to allow direct comparison between courses at different HEIs. Perhaps most importantly these results affect an institution's position in the league tables for HEIs, which are published by several national newspapers and by the *Times Higher Education Supplement*. As a consequence of their high profile and influence, NSS results have led to significant changes in the way courses are organised at many institutions. Increasingly, institutions are creating structures and functions that are directly determined by the NSS. Again, whether as a tutor or manager involved with HE, you need to be aware of the NSS.

As with other quality assurance procedures, the scope of the NSS depends upon funding: it only applies to courses funded through HEFCE.

There are 23 core questions that relate to the following eight aspects of the student learning experience:

1. Teaching on My Course
2. Assessment and Feedback
3. Academic Support
4. Organisation and Management
5. Learning Resources
6. Personal Development
7. Overall Satisfaction
8. Students' Union (Association or Guild)

Tutors are expressly forbidden from actively influencing their students' responses to the NSS; to do so might be considered gross misconduct. Nevertheless, the NSS is controversial. Some consider the questions to be reductive; some think the survey might persuade tutors to be less challenging of their students; and on small courses, such as in many FE colleges, one or two students might make a disproportionate difference to the overall percentages. A senior academic at Lancaster University who has studied the impact of the NSS on institutional behaviour told the *Times Higher Education Supplement* in September 2102 that an increased focus on the survey could distract institutions from more meaningful ways to improve courses: if you put in place a measure and call it a 'performance indicator', people will feel the need to improve those scores even at the expense of other activities that will have a larger impact on student experience. Nonetheless, the government sets great store on the NSS and therefore so do HEIs who will often have strategies to enhance their scores. You need to be aware of the NSS and any results relevant to your HE course. You may well be asked to make specific reference to the NSS and how you will improve your results in the annual course review document.

BEFLECTIVE TASK

REFLECTIVE TASK

Before reading on, spend a few moments thinking about a course you have been on as a student in the past. How would you judge the quality of that course? What criteria did you use? How, if at all, were you able to inform or influence the course? How has your experience of being a student informed your role as a teacher or manager?

Professional Standards

The Higher Education Academy (HEA) has some of the same roles as the Institute for Learning (IfL) in FE, but unlike the IfL there has never been a statutory obligation for HE staff to join. That said, many universities now require that their staff join the HEA, just as they require staff to have a teaching qualification (or to work towards one if they do not). You should check just what is required by any HEI with which you are collaborating. The HEA is funded by the four UK national HE funding bodies and by subscriptions and grants and it *champions excellent learning and teaching in higher education* (www.heacademy.ac.uk). It also has a responsibility *to enhance the quality and impact of learning and teaching... by recognising and rewarding excellent teaching, bringing together people and resources to research and share best practice, and by helping to influence, shape and implement policy* (ibid.) Part of this responsibility involves publishing the professional standards for HE staff. The difference between the professional standards for staff teaching HE courses and for staff teaching FE courses is, arguably, illustrative of the different attitude the government has had towards the two sectors. The LLUK standards, which came into statutory force in 2007 and which are currently under review, are 20 pages long, have six domains and dozens of statements that describe what is expected of teachers in the Learning and Skills Sector. The comparable standards produced by the HEA are not statutory and amount to a mere four pages and contain around 20 broad statements covering professional practice. Lea and Simmons (2012, page 183) suggest that these *two systems could be argued to prepare people perfectly for either a managerial or a more collegial culture*. As we said at the beginning of this chapter, however, these two systems are not as distinct as they were in the past. In any case, while you are teaching on an HE course, it is the HEA Professional Standards Framework that is relevant.

> *At the heart of this framework is acknowledgement of the distinctive nature of teaching in higher education, respect for the autonomy of higher education institutions, and recognition of the sector's understanding of quality enhancement for improving student learning. The framework recognises that the scholarly nature of subject inquiry and knowledge creation, and a scholarly approach to pedagogy, combine to represent a unique feature of support for student learning in higher education institutions.*

(Higher Education Academy, 2012, page 2)

Some FE tutors will find this approach refreshing and in pleasing contrast to the tone of much of what pertains to other courses taught in their sector.

Responsibilities differ across HE in FE provision. So, find the answers to these questions in relation to your course. Are the students subject to the procedures (such as those for equal opportunities, complaints and disciplinary issues) of the college or the university (or other awarding body)? To make this more concrete, if a student is suspected of plagiarism, who carries out the formal investigation?

External examination

External examination once again comes under the remit of QAA, and its Quality Code (as discussed in Chapter 7) has five indicators that pertain to external examiners. The second indicator sets out the role of the external examiner (very often referred to as 'the external')

Awarding institutions expect their external examiners to provide informative comment and recommendations upon whether or not:

an institution is maintaining the threshold academic standards set for its awards in accordance with the frameworks for higher education qualifications and applicable subject benchmark statements

the assessment process measures student achievement rigorously and fairly against the intended outcomes of the programme(s) and is conducted in line with the institution's policies and regulations

the academic standards and the achievements of students are comparable with those in other UK higher education institutions of which the external examiners have experience.

So, the external examiner's function is to check standards on a course but also to advise the course team on the future development of a course.

In many respects, then, external examiners have a similar role to external verifiers on many FE courses. The reports they write, however, differ in so far as in HE these are based upon the examiners' professional judgement and, while they will have specific areas to look at, examiners' reports are generally not tied to specific criteria. Examiners' reports can, therefore, be as particular or as wide-ranging as the examiner sees fit.

The course leader or the course team select examiners and before appointment their suitability has to be verified by the HEI's body with responsibility for assessment, such as the teaching and learning committee and registry. An external examiner needs to be suitably qualified and experienced in the appropriate area. They will often be an academic from another university, but commonly vocational courses also have representatives from the profession. Regulations vary, but to avoid conflicts of interest examiners typically must have had no recent relationship with the HEI where the course is run and the period of their duties is limited, typically to around three years.

A close relationship between examiner and course team can be crucial to a course's continuing success. Examiners remain very powerful since any comments or criticisms they make have to be specifically and demonstrably addressed by the course team. Very often they have to be consulted on changes to the course, but their role in assessment is most apparent. The precise responsibility of the examiner will vary between institutions and courses; even the number of examiners for any provision can vary substantially. On one course examiners may share responsibility for looking at all the modules; on another course each examiner may have responsibility for a particular module or area of the course. Examiners have access to students' work, which may be sent to them to assess, or a sample will be available when they visit. Normally examiners will have the opportunity to speak to students as well as to the course team when they visit the HEI. These visits often coincide with the course assessment board when credits and awards are formally made to students because external examiners have a duty to oversee these boards and their decisions.

At the beginning of this chapter we made the point that what has been termed the audit culture, which has existed for some time in FE, has begun to spread to HE. The role of the external examiner is, however, characteristic of an older collegiality based upon professional trust and it has been identified as central to the success of HE provision in the UK.

PRACTICAL TASK PRACTICAL TASK **PRACTICAL TASK** PRACTICAL TASK **PRACTICAL TASK**

Find out if your course has external examiners. If so, who are they? What are their relevant qualifications and experience? For which elements of the course do they have responsibility? How would you like them to help you develop your own practice or provision?

Some points to consider when working with university and college quality systems

FE organisations are typically very used to forming strong and positive working relationships with partners in industry, local government or schools. Similarly, relationships between FEIs and the HEIs with which they co-operate are generally good. There has been considerable competition to attract FE partners because these relationships can be lucrative for HEIs, though in recent years some universities have pulled out of their collaborative provision occasionally with very short notice leaving their former partners in the lurch. Many FEIs work with several partners in their HE provision and these partners may change according to the 'value-for-money' they offer to colleges or in response to demands for new courses. The form of the partnership relationship is also a consideration: a consortium arrangement is perhaps more consensual and may allow the FEI more control, but there may be more administrative burden. On the other hand, franchise arrangements may be more straightforward, but colleges may be more vulnerable to the HEI making changes to their courses. The precise arrangement between the two partners is set out in the formal partnership agreement or memorandum of collaboration, which covers financial and legal responsibilities. Frequently, however, those actually involved in managing and teaching the courses mentioned in these documents have never seen them.

Though broadly similar, the validation and other quality procedures for particular HEIs differ, so there are difficulties with having too many partners. Multiple partners mean multiple systems. Above all, it is crucial to be clear about exactly what your partner

HEI requires and when. Most HEIs will have a named link or liaison tutor who is the main link between the HEI and the FE partner. Some partnerships require attendance at regular meetings at the HEI, even every month. All require tutors' attendance at moderation events, course committees and assessment boards where credits are awarded. Senior college managers may also need to attend steering groups or committees.

Find answers to the following questions about your own provision to help ensure that you know what you need to.

- Are you clear about your role and responsibilities as well as those of your colleagues and institution? Who is your link tutor?
- Who has overall responsibility for quality?
- Who can you contact if you have a query or problem?
- How are you involved in developing the curriculum?
- Do you understand the funding arrangement and what funding, if any, you may use for resources?
- Do you have a calendar of events and deadlines that specifies your obligations to your partner organisation? This would cover regular meetings, assignment submission dates, external examiners' visits and so on.
- If you are involved with more than one HE awarding body, how exactly do their procedures differ?

Preparing documentation for quality assurance purposes

You should receive clear guidance on what precisely is required by your HE partner so the following are only a guide. Validation events for courses involve a great deal of documentation so you will need to be clear about what the partner HEI or awarding body expects. Re-validation every three to five years, dependent on the agreement, is similar. The following list is typical of what might be required:

- A broad description of your institution and its setting.
- An account of any prior relationship with the HEI and any other experience of HE provision.
- A description of the current and anticipated demand for the course along with some evidence for this demand.
- A description of the resources available for the HE provision at the institution. This would include the rooms used for classes, IT resources as well as the staff delivering the course. Often the partner will want to see CVs.
- Proposals for how the course will be delivered and how students will be supported.
- For re-validation, data relating to student retention and achievement may be required.
- Procedures to ensure quality assurance and for how the provision will be managed more generally. This may entail describing how your institution will adapt existing processes to meet the partner's requirements.
- Copies of any existing or proposed publicity material for the provision under consideration.
- Other information relevant to the provision.

Every year, in addition, the FEI will need to produce for its HE partner some form of self-assessment report or annual evaluation document that covers the relevant information. This document may include data detailing student retention and achievement; the destination of completing students; demand for the course; and so on. It will require the identification of strengths and how any weaknesses will be addressed; often this document will ask for specific reference to external examiners' reports or the NSS.

Producing the self-evaluation document for Review of College Higher Education

As we have seen above this procedure to investigate collaborative provision is new. The QAA has produced *Guidelines for producing the self-evaluation document for Review of College Higher Education (RCHE)* available at: www.qaa.ac.uk/InstitutionReports/types-of-review/RCHE/Documents/RCHE-SED-guidelines.pdf.

This self-evaluation document (SED) is of particular importance because the length of the review to which an institution will be subject depends on the quality and focus of this document. Get it right and you will have a shorter review. The first page of the QAA's guidelines (ibid) states: *the better targeted the SED is to the areas of the review, the more carefully chosen the evidence, and the more reflective the document is, the greater the likelihood that the team will be able to verify your college's approaches and gather evidence of its own quickly and effectively*.

The guidelines recommend that the information required in the SED be set out under a total of four *judgement headings*, each of which in effect comprises a sentence to be completed as appropriate according to the result of the investigation. The four judgement sentences, and the possible results, are as follows:

- Judgement 1. The academic standards of the awards the college offers on behalf of its awarding bodies…
- Possible results. There are two possible results: *either* '…meet UK expectations for threshold standards' *or* '…do not meet UK expectations for threshold standards'.
- Judgement 2: The quality of student learning opportunities…
- Judgement 3: The quality of the information produced by the college about its learning opportunities…
- Judgement 4: The enhancement of student learning opportunities…
- Possible results. Judgements 2, 3 and 4 are all graded according to one of four outcomes:

  - '…is commended'
  - '…meets UK expectations'
  - '…requires improvement to meet UK expectations'
  - '…does not meet UK expectations'.

Here is the basic structure for the SED for RCHE that the QAA suggests in the guidelines.

(A) Core elements of the review:

Section 1: Brief description of the college

Section 2: How the college has addressed the recommendations of its last review(s)

Section 3: The college's threshold academic standards

Section 4: The quality of students' learning opportunities (teaching and academic support)

Section 5: The quality of public information, including that produced for students and applicants

Section 6: The college's enhancement of students' learning opportunities

(B) Thematic element of review:

Here you will address the required specific theme or themes. Examples include:

- innovations in student involvement in quality
- student contributions to enhancement
- staff experience of/participation in student involvement in quality

Remember, all of this is subject to change and so it is imperative that you keep up to date with the current requirements of your partner institution and any agency involved.

So, what does all this quality assurance tell us about HE in FE?

In 2006 the HEFCE specifically noted that FE colleges were better than HE generally at reaching out to learners and HE in FE also scores well for supporting mature students on part-time courses. More recently the extensive report written for the government by Gareth Parry and his team found the following:

> In terms of the multiple forms of evidence available there appears to be little ground for general concern about academic quality and standards with regard to HE provision in FECs. This is generally confirmed by our sample of colleges. Both reports of Ofsted inspections (although their direct relevance to HE provision can be questioned) and IQERs by the Quality Assurance Agency are generally complimentary. Prompt action is taken on any areas of concerns/ for improvement that are identified. Relations with validating universities are generally good.... Relationships between HEI and FEC staff appear to be collegial and developmental. Remarkably perhaps, there appears to be little resentment of these multiple layers of scrutiny.

(Parry et al., 2012, page 91)

Professional HE in FE courses are often taught by people with recent experience of the workplace with which they retain close ties, meaning that their specialist knowledge is current. FE teachers may be more available to meet students than HE lecturers, and many FE teachers have a professional ethos based around pastoral care for their students. All of this highlights what may be perceived as strengths of HE in FE and the benefits for students of, for example, taking their degree at a college. There are some general weaknesses across the sector, though, and some FE settings struggle to provide what Lea and Simmons (2012) have referred to as *HEness* or the distinctive culture of an HEI. This varies greatly. Some large colleges like Grimsby Institute of Further and Higher Education have a separate HE building with dedicated facilities; Manchester College concentrates its HE provision in a separate campus; but in many colleges HE and FE provision may be in the same space and taught by the same teachers with little apparent differentiation. FE teachers are paid less than their counterparts in universities, have far more contact time over the year and often less administrative support. As a consequence FE teachers have little time for scholarship or research, which for many is a component of *HEness*. Indeed, some would argue that the culture of support for students that is celebrated in many FE organisations may constitute a reduced *therapeutic education* which infantilises students rather than challenging them intellectually (see Ecclestone and Hayes, 2009). This criticism may be levelled against some HEIs, too. Certainly, though, few colleges can match the resources of universities.

What can be done to bolster the quality of HE in FE?

Philip Davies (2007, pages 48–9) from Bournemouth and Poole College has identified some elements that should be considered in relation to quality assurance.

- A distinctive HE environment: separate facilities designated for HE students with their own communal areas.
- Reduction in staff loading: while acknowledging the difficulties in addressing this, Davies argues that *staff loading is directly linked to quality.*
- Support for scholarly activity/research: some colleges have modest funds available for these activities; some have produced their own journals to publicise their research activities; and others have research events.
- A separate and dedicated quality system: some FEIs have no apparent difficulty in marrying the two quality systems or running them concurrently. A separate and distinctive set of procedures may be more beneficial, however.
- Support for specific HE staff development: it is generally accepted that staff should normally be qualified to the level above that which they teach and that is also true of HE. That would mean FEIs supporting their HE staff to gain the appropriate qualifications by paying for courses and allowing sufficient time for study.

Davies makes an important point: FEIs cannot compete with HEIs as if they were equal. Rather, FEIs with HE provision should focus on what they are good at, which for many will be providing vocationally focused courses or attracting students who traditionally have never benefited from any HE. Nonetheless, there is evidence that FE in HE really does place the student at the centre of considerations.

REFLECTIVE TASK

Think about your own experience of HE as a student and as a tutor. What do you consider 'HEness' to be? What different expectations do students have of HE courses? How do you differentiate your own HE sessions from other provision at a lower level? What would help you to achieve a greater distinctiveness between FE and HE courses?

A SUMMARY OF KEY POINTS

During this chapter we have looked at the following key issues:
- Quality assurance procedures in HE are diverse and subject to frequent change.
- The crucial importance of remaining informed about any changes.
- The role of the QAA.
- The role of external examiners.
- The quality of HE provision in FE.

Quality assurance can be mystifying to the inexperienced lecturer, but there is a great deal of guidance on this available from the QAA and Ofsted on their websites. Moreover, the HE partners we work with will also have their own guidance documentation. Quality assurance, and the administrative work that goes with it, is an ever-present aspect of the works of the HE lecturer – both in colleges and in universities. Some lecturers will always complain about the need to engage with quality systems, but they are – rightly or wrongly – an unavoidable aspect of contemporary academic life.

Branching options

Reflection

What are the expectations placed on you by the different quality systems that you are required to work with? Are there different systems – such as those required by a college as distinct from those required by a franchising university – to manage? Do these complement or contradict each other?

Analysis

What is the relationship between the kinds of work required for quality assurance as discussed in this chapter, and your teaching, or other academic work? Does QA seem to occupy an unduly prominent position in your work, or in the work of your colleagues? If so, why might this be? Or is QA something that you do not need to engage with?

Research

The impact of quality assurance and managerialism continues to be a topic for research and debate in HE (as also discussed in the preceding chapter). The articles and books referenced at the end of this chapter (as well as Chapter 8) provide a good introduction to this area of work.

REFERENCES REFERENCES REFERENCES REFERENCES REFERENCES

Davies, P. (2007) HE in FE: the struggle for excellence, *Academy Exchange,* 7: 48–9.

Ecclestone, K. and Hayes, D. (2009) *The Dangerous Rise of Therapeutic Education.* London: Routledge.

HEA *(2012) HEA UK Professional Standards Framework.* Available online at: www.heacademy. ac.uk/ukpsf (accessed 03/06/13).

Lea, J. and Simmons, J. (2012) Higher education in further education: capturing and promoting HEness, *Research in Post-Compulsory Education,* 17 (2): 179–93.

Lifelong Learning UK (2006) *New Overarching Professional Standards for Teachers, Tutors and Trainers in the Lifelong Learning Sector.* London: Lifelong Learning UK.

Parry, G., Callender, C., Scott, P. and Temple, P. (2012) *BIS Research Paper number 69: Understanding Higher Education in Further Education Institutions.* London: DBIS.

QAA (2007) *Education Studies.* Available online at: www.qaa.ac.uk/Publications/ InformationAndGuidance/Documents/Education07.pdf (accessed 06/08/13).

QAA, *UK Quality Code for Higher Education* available online at: www.qaa.ac.uk/AssuringStandards AndQuality/Pages/default.aspx (accessed 03/06/13).

QAA, *Guidelines for Producing the Self-Evaluation Document for Review of College Higher Education (RCHE)* available online at: www.qaa.ac.uk/InstitutionReports/types-of-review/RCHE/ Documents/RCHE-SED-guidelines.pdf (accessed 03/06/13).

Stanton, G. (2009) A view from within the English further education sector on the provision of higher education: Issues of verticality and agency, *Higher Education Quarterly,* 63 (4): 419–33.

Index